HARMONY

STRUCTURE
AND STYLE

MCGRAW-HILL SERIES IN MUSIC
William J. Mitchell, *Consulting Editor*

ATKISSON: *Basic Counterpoint*

CHASE: *America's Music*

CROCKER: *A History of Musical Style*

RATNER: *Harmony: Structure and Style*

RATNER: *Music: The Listener's Art*

WAGNER: *Band Scoring*

HARMONY
STRUCTURE
AND STYLE

LEONARD G. RATNER   *Professor of Music*
Stanford University

McGraw-Hill Book Company, Inc.   *New York   San Francisco   Toronto   London*

HARMONY: STRUCTURE AND STYLE

Library of Congress Catalog Card Number 62-10851

ISBN 07-051213-2

890 HDBP 7543

Preface

When we listen to music, we hear its elements within a general plan of musical action. We may recognize the presence of a certain chord, its position and spacing, but we hear the chord as part of a larger context. If harmony, or, for that matter, any aspect of musical composition, is to be understood properly, it should be presented as an element in musical expression and form. This book endeavors to present harmony in such a light.

In order to associate harmony with musical expression, some significant modifications of the traditional methods of presentation have been made in this book. Traditional methods generally place emphasis upon chord vocabulary, worked out in a four-part choral texture. In this book, we have incorporated each chord or procedure, as soon as it is presented, into some plan of musical structure and composition. When harmony is presented in such a context, it has strong and immediate meaning to the student; when he understands the relation of the harmonic item to the full musical process, he is challenged to try his creative imagery upon the materials at hand.

We have presented musical materials and processes so as to channel the student's activity eventually toward composition and analysis. This presentation leads to an organization of basic concepts in the following sequence: (1) the *definition of key* as embodied in (2) *cadential formulas* organized into (3) *phrases and periods,* which are given rhetorical and expressive value by (4) *rhythmic, melodic, and textural elaboration* reflecting various characteristic styles. Musical structure is expanded by (5) *nonfinal cadences and expanded cadential action.* Larger-scale musical structure is organized by (6) *plans of modulation.*

In Western music this scheme of organization is most clearly embodied in music of the late eighteenth and early nineteenth centuries. Hence, the majority of the examples in this book are drawn from the music of Haydn, Mozart, Beethoven, Schubert, Mendelssohn, and Chopin.

Materials usually covered in harmony textbooks are treated in the course of this book. However, the order of presentation and the explanations are directed to studies in rhythmic elaboration, melodic design, exploration of texture, and the building of musical form.

In order to proceed directly to the creative work which is the focus of this presentation, we begin with musical intervals which we organize into cadential formulas and then elaborate with characteristic rhythmic and melodic figures. Thus we establish for the entire study a basic texture of two voices, corresponding to soprano and bass. Such a two-voice texture permits flexibility in melodic action, avoids the "traffic jams" that arise when the student first tries to make four voices march along properly; it invites the student to try some creative work; moreover, it draws the student's attention to the essential elements in a musical texture, i.e., the historically important opposition of soprano and bass. Since it is these voices which take the lead in musical action, special attention given to them in theory work will prove most beneficial in analysis and performance.

Elaboration of all kinds is the process by which the harmonic language is here presented: (1) a simple vocabulary becomes elaborated with fuller and richer chord types; (2) cadential formulas are elaborated into phrases and periods; (3) motives are elaborated into melodies; (4) diatonic cadential action is elaborated by secondary dominants and by modulation; (5) a sonority sufficient only to carry forward harmonic action is elaborated into a full texture with distinctive color qualities; (6) simple phrases and periods are elaborated into extended periods and small complete forms. In each of these processes there is an organic growth from a simple to a more highly developed procedure.

This enables us to present material so that at any given time during the course of study the student has a balanced, coordinated musical language with which to test his creativity. Often, he will be asked to use exercises which he has already composed in order to build larger musical structures. Thus, he can enjoy the growth of the complex from the simple and, at the same time, refine his materials through a growing sense of musical taste.

In this approach certain topics are critical. These are the sense of key, the cadential formula, rhythmic and melodic elaboration, and the period. Regardless of the order of presentation which the individual instructor may find suitable to a given set of circumstances, it is recommended that these topics remain central and be referred to as the bases of all further work.

The exercises at the end of each chapter provide the following:

1. Ear training
2. Specific writing drill
3. Incorporation of the material into creative writing
4. Analysis of the procedure in question in examples drawn from music literature

This book should cover the first two years of music-theory study beyond the preliminary work in ear training, sight singing, etc. Parts 1 and 2 deal with the structural aspects of tonal harmony as defined in music of the eighteenth and early nineteenth centuries. Part 3 introduces the student to some characteristic aspects of coloristic harmony as practiced in the nineteenth century; however, this area of harmony is interpreted mainly as an extension of the traditional treatment of sonority and action.

The harmonic styles covered in this book range from a simple dance and song style typical of the mid- and late eighteenth century through more elaborate techniques as might be found in the sonatas of the classical masters, the songs of Schubert, and the piano music of Mendelssohn and Chopin to the rich chromatic language of the mid-nineteenth century.

Indeed, the entire approach takes into account where and how a procedure is employed, as well as what it may be. In order to do this properly, the structures in which these procedures find a proper "habitat" are described, and the relationship between harmonic "climate" and musical form is explained.

During the course of study many procedures of part writing related to free counterpoint will be employed. These are not intended to duplicate or supersede the study of counterpoint, since they are associated with harmonic and rhythmic action. The study of counterpoint is a specialized discipline based on musical structures different from those we are considering here. Yet, the materials and procedures embodied in this text should prove useful when the study of counterpoint is undertaken.

For the work here, the student should have some facility at the piano. He should know scales, chords, key signatures, time signatures. For the present approach, sensitivity to interval sound is essential, since much harmonic action derives from interval relationships and interaction. We begin, therefore, with a review of the structure and qualities of intervals.

Leonard Ratner

Contents

Part One

Harmonic Sonorities

Chapter One

Intervals

One musical sound sets one level of pitch. Two musical sounds heard together or in close succession combine to mark off an *interval;* an interval consists of the *distance* between the pitch levels of two tones.

For the listener, intervals have two general aspects:

1. The *size,* or *extent,* of the interval; this refers to the distance in pitch encompassed by the two tones.

2. The *effect* of the interval; this refers to the quality of sound, or tone color, created by the interaction of the two tones. Each interval has its own distinctive quality, or effect, so much so that we can recognize different intervals much more easily by their respective effects than by measuring the exact distance between the tones.

In this chapter we shall refer both to the specific compass of intervals and to some of the general effects which their qualities, by common usage, seem to project in music of the Western tradition. Such effects and qualities tend to be valued subjectively; still, we can observe such consistencies in treatment that it would be unrealistic to overlook these effects or to minimize them. When intervals are combined with each other or are very large or are placed in extremely high or low registers, their effects may be different from those described in this chapter, which apply only to intervals sounded *alone* and in a *middle* register.

Mutual relationships of tones, as expressed in the *qualities* and *effects* of various intervals, constitute the basis of harmony in Western music. These relationships may be placed in operation regardless of pitch, color, or combination. Composers of the eighteenth and nineteenth centuries have consistently chosen to employ intervallic qualities and relationships so as to build a clearly logical plan of harmonic action. In order to explore this system we should understand some of the implications for color and action that emerge from the nature of musical intervals.

When tones are heard in succession, they are commonly said to create a *melodic* interval; when they are heard simultaneously, they are described as creating a *harmonic* interval. This latter designation has been used because of the general notion that harmony is built out of simultaneous sounds. While this is not entirely correct, as we shall see throughout this book, the term *harmonic* is sufficiently clear in this meaning to be acceptable.

3

4

CLASSIFICATION OF INTERVALS

An interval is described, further, in two ways:

1. According to the number of degrees on the musical staff that it encompasses; this is a numerical designation.

EX. 1.   Numerical designation of intervals

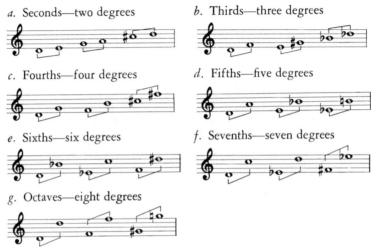

a. Seconds—two degrees

b. Thirds—three degrees

c. Fourths—four degrees

d. Fifths—five degrees

e. Sixths—six degrees

f. Sevenths—seven degrees

g. Octaves—eight degrees

2. According to its exact size. Intervals of the same numerical designation, such as seconds or thirds, may differ somewhat in size and sound according to the position on the staff which they occupy. Alterations, such as sharps, flats, and natural signs, also affect the size of intervals. The following terms are used to account for the variations in interval size:

    a. Perfect. Applied to unisons, fourths, fifths, and octaves. Any increase or decrease in the size of perfect intervals causes a drastic change of character in their sound quality.

    b. Major, minor. Applied to seconds, thirds, sixths, and sevenths. Major intervals are one half step larger than minor intervals. A major interval may be decreased in size to minor, or vice versa, without loss of the general sound quality associated with the numerical type, i.e., seconds, thirds, etc. Major and minor intervals represent variations of shade within a given color value. This we shall examine in detail below.

    c. Augmented. Applied to intervals one half step larger than major or perfect intervals.

    d. Diminished. Applied to intervals one half step smaller than perfect or minor.

Below we have listed the intervals contained in the octave, their compass in half steps and whole steps, a brief description of their qualities, and examples of their use in musical literature. Thirds and larger intervals may be arranged in several different ways with respect to their internal distribution of whole steps and half steps. These alternative arrangements do not affect the actual size of a given interval.

1. *Unison.* Two voices singing the same pitch sing a *unison.* This generally refers to a harmonic interval. If a voice remains at the same pitch in a melodic line, it is repeating the tone at the unison.

EX. 2.   Unisons, harmonic and melodic

a. Harmonic unison   *b.* Melodic unison (repeated tone)

2. *Minor second.* One half step, involving different staff degrees. The minor second is a tight, binding interval, either rising or falling. We have the feeling that the two tones involved in the minor second are pulling at each other. This relationship has given rise to what has been called *leading-tone* action, an action which has been of tremendous importance in the harmonic language of the past five hundred years.

EX. 3.   The minor second

a. Notation of the minor second

b. Melodic use of the minor second

Beethoven: Grosse Fuge, Op. 133   Mozart: Sonata in F major, K. 332, first movement

c. Harmonic use of the minor second

Mozart: Sonata in A minor, K. 310, first movement

Harmonically, the minor second creates a sharp edgy clash.

In our present harmonic system, there is another interval that consists of a half step, the *augmented unison,* or, as it is more often called, the *chromatic half step.* Like the minor second, the chromatic half step gives the impression of closeness of movement in a melodic line. However, in the language of harmony, the chromatic half step has the value of an *inflection* of a previous tone, rather than of a direct progression *forward* which the minor second projects.

EX. 4.   Chromatic half step

a. Notation of the chromatic half step

b. Melodic use of the chromatic half step

Mozart: Quintet in E♭ major, K. 614, second movement

Beethoven: Quartet in C major, Op. 59, no. 3, first movement

3. *Major second.* One whole step.

EX. 5.   The major second

a. Notation of the major second

b. Melodic use of the major second

Brahms: Symphony No. 2, Op. 73, first movement

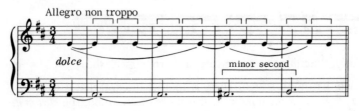

c. Harmonic use of the major second

Beethoven: Sonata in C minor, Op. 10, no. 1, first movement

Note the difference in effect between the minor seconds and the major seconds in the above examples. The major second seems to be less binding in its melodic action. Below are given three melodies, similar in outline but different in their use of seconds. The first is composed entirely of half steps, the second entirely of whole steps, while the third contains both half and whole steps. Neither of the first two melodies possesses the balance of effect which we find in the third melody. The half steps in the third melody create a contrast with the whole steps and establish points of reference which enable the listener to sense an inner control; this control we shall later recognize as the sense of key, or tonal center.

EX. 6.   Melodies built on seconds

a. Minor seconds and chromatic half steps

b. Major seconds

c. Mixture of major and minor seconds

4. *Augmented second.* One and one half steps, notated on adjacent scale degrees. This interval in a melody gives the impression of being conjunct but only barely so; since it is so large, it is quite difficult to sing or play in tune. Nevertheless, it creates a striking effect and, because of its size, may impart a somewhat uneven quality of movement to a melody in which it appears.

EX. 7.   The augmented second

a. Notation of the augmented second

b. Melodic use of the augmented second

Beethoven: Sonata in C minor, Op. 10, no. 1, first movement

Mozart: Quartet in D minor, K. 421, finale

5. *Major and minor thirds.* The major third consists of two whole steps; the minor third, of one and one half steps. Since Renaissance times major and minor thirds have constituted two of the chief ingredients in the construction of chords. Both the major and the minor third produce effects of fullness, richness, and euphony, giving an impression of smooth blend. This is particularly the case when thirds are sounded harmonically. Major and minor thirds have often been set in opposition to each other to create striking shifts of color. This is because the major third sounds markedly brighter and more assertive than the minor third.

EX. 8.   Major and minor thirds

a. Notation of major and minor thirds

b. Melodic use of major and minor thirds

Beethoven: Symphony No. 3, Op. 55, finale

c. Harmonic use of major and minor thirds

Note, in the harmonic example, the contrast in effect that occurred when the shift from major third to minor third or vice versa was made. The difference between the thirds is probably more striking in harmonic intervals than in melodic intervals.

6. *Diminished third*. Two half steps, notated on adjacent spaces or lines. The diminished third, sometimes used in a melody, sounds like the major second but will suggest, in spite of its narrowness, a disjunct melodic progression. The diminished third exploits the binding quality of two minor seconds.

EX. 9.   Diminished third

a. Notation of the diminished third

b. Melodic use of the diminished third

Mozart: Fantasia in C minor, K. 475

7. *Perfect fourth*. Two and one half steps. Melodically, this is a bold, open interval which gives, like the perfect fifth (see below), an effect of strength and firmness to a melody. Harmonically, the fourth has the same open quality but in certain cases creates an impression of instability.

EX. 10.   The perfect fourth

a. Notation of the perfect fourth

b. Melodic use of the perfect fourth

Mendelssohn: *A Midsummer Night's Dream*, Nocturne   Wagner: *The Flying Dutchman*, Overture

c. Harmonic use of the perfect fourth

8. *Augmented fourth*. Three whole steps. Melodically, the augmented fourth seems to convey a tense, unstable, and somewhat awkward effect. Harmonically, the specific tension value of this interval gives it a unique importance in harmonic action.

EX. 11.   The augmented fourth

a. Notation of the augmented fourth

b. Melodic use of the augmented fourth

Brahms: Symphony No. 1, Op. 68, first movement

c. Harmonic use of the augmented fourth

Mozart: Quintet in E♭ major, K. 614, finale

9. *Perfect fifth.* Three whole steps, one half step. Like the fourth, this is a powerful and stable interval when used in a melody. The strength and firmness of the fifth is even greater when it is used as a harmonic interval.

EX. 12.   The perfect fifth

a. Notation of the perfect fifth

b. Melodic use of the perfect fifth

Beethoven: Symphony No. 3, Op. 55, finale

c. Harmonic use of the perfect fifth

Beethoven: Symphony No. 9, Op. 125, first movement

10. *Diminished fifth.* Two whole steps, two half steps. In sound, this interval is identical to the augmented fourth. In a melody, the diminished fifth is generally negotiated more easily than the augmented fourth; harmonically, the two intervals are virtually equivalent in effect.

EX. 13.   The diminished fifth

a. Notation of the diminished fifth

b. Melodic use of the diminished fifth

Schubert: Quintet in C major, Op. 163, finale

c. Harmonic use of the diminished fifth

Mozart: Sonata in C minor, K. 457, second movement

11. *Augmented fifth.* Four whole steps. Sounded by itself, this interval does not appear unstable; however, in a melodic line or a harmonic progression it gives an unstable but not harsh effect to the music. This interval has exactly the same sound as the minor sixth, but, because of its relationship with other tones, the augmented fifth has a somewhat uncertain sound, while the minor sixth seems to have a firmer anchorage.

EX. 14.   The augmented fifth

a. Notation of the augmented fifth

b. Harmonic use of the augmented fifth

Beethoven: Grosse Fuge, Op. 133

c. Harmonic use of the augmented fifth

Schubert: Quintet in C major, Op. 163, first movement

12. *Major and minor sixths.* The major sixth consists of four whole steps and one half step; the minor sixth, of three whole steps and two half steps. Sixths, like thirds, have a fullness and sweetness of sound, particularly in harmonic intervals, that is quite satisfying and often sufficient as a complete musical sonority. This is demonstrated in Exs. 8*b* and 15*b,* where we hear two voices proceeding in thirds and sixths, respectively.

EX. 15.   Major and minor sixths

a. Notation of major and minor sixths

b. Melodic use of major and minor sixths

Mozart: Sonata in F major, K. 332, finale

c. Harmonic use of major and minor sixths

Mozart: Fantasia in C minor, K. 475

13. *Augmented sixth.* Five whole steps or four whole steps and two half steps. In musical practice this is used almost exclusively as a harmonic interval.

EX. 16.   The augmented sixth

a. Notation of the augmented sixth

b. Harmonic use of the augmented sixth

Mozart: Fantasia in C minor, K. 475

14. *Major and minor sevenths.* The major seventh consists of five whole steps and one half step; the minor seventh, of four whole steps and two half steps. Sevenths, major and minor, have in common a wide, unsteady effect as melodic intervals, the major seventh more so than the minor. As harmonic intervals, both sevenths have a rather harsh, unblended quality, the major more than the minor.

EX. 17.   Major and minor sevenths

a. Notation of major and minor sevenths

b. Melodic use of major and minor sevenths

Mozart: Sonata in D major, K. 576, finale

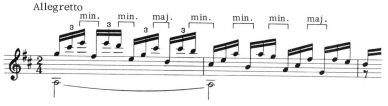

c. Harmonic use of major and minor sevenths

Mozart: Sonata in D major, K. 576, first movement

15. *Diminished seventh.* Three whole steps and three half steps. In sound, this interval resembles the major sixth, but in the following example we can hear that it imparts tension to the melody. Melodically, this interval has a very great potential for the expression of a dramatic or pathetic value.

EX. 18.   The diminished seventh

a. Notation of the diminished seventh

b. Harmonic and melodic use of the diminished seventh

Mozart: Sonata in C minor, K. 457, finale

16. *Octave.* The octave represents the duplication of a tone on two levels, five whole steps and two half steps apart. Since this is a duplication, the interval of the octave is much easier to sing than some smaller intervals,

such as the augmented fourth, diminished third, or major sixth. Harmonically, the two tones of the octave merge so well that it is often difficult to
distinguish them. The octave, both harmonically and melodically, has a
wide, open, yet steady and firm effect.

EX. 19. The octave

a. Notation of the octave

b. Harmonic and.melodic use of the octave

Beethoven: Sonata in D major, Op. 10, no. 3, second movement

   The effects of musical intervals which have been described in this chapter
apply particularly to intervals heard by themselves, out of a musical context.
Within a context the effects may be intensified, modified, indeed, canceled,
or reversed by combinations with other tones, rhythmic action, orchestration,
and pitch levels. Thus, a perfect fifth may well become part of a very unstable combination of tones, or in a melody the perfect fifth may be unable
to assert its stability because of surrounding circumstances. Still, each interval may impart some of its character to a chord or to a melody; this may
actually become one of the means by which the composer controls the
sound of his music. Music which uses one kind of interval prominently and
frequently, such as minor seconds, major thirds, perfect fourths, or sevenths,
will have a general quality of sound that can be referred to the specific effect
of the chosen interval.
   We have dealt rather extensively with intervals because they are the
building blocks for harmonic structure and furnish the power for harmonic
action. We must be able to hear intervals and appreciate their qualities in
order to work in musical composition. This review of intervals has, thus,
served two purposes:

   1. To fix the sound and the notation of intervals for the student
   2. To prepare for the work to follow, which will take its point of departure
from interval relationships

Interval	Size	Effect
Unison		Melodic—repetition; harmonic—duplication
Minor second	One half step	Melodic—tight, binding; harmonic—clashing, close, edgy
Major second	One whole step	Melodic—smooth, conjunct; harmonic—less clash than minor second
Chromatic half step	One half step	Melodic—closeness of movement, alteration of previous tone
Augmented second	One whole step, one half step	Melodic—widest possible effect of conjunct movement
Minor third	One whole step, one half step	Melodic—small, easy skip; harmonic—euphonious, rather dark
Major third	Two whole steps	Melodic—small, easy skip; harmonic—euphonious, brighter than minor third
Diminished third	Two half steps	Melodic—effect of narrowness and compression, yet disjunct; harmonic—similar to major second when heard alone
Perfect fourth	Two whole steps, one half step	Melodic—firm, open leap; harmonic—open but unstable
Augmented fourth	Three whole steps	Melodic—awkward leap; harmonic—unstable, effect of tension
Diminished fifth	Two whole steps, two half steps	Melodic—effect of tightness; harmonic—unstable, tense
Perfect fifth	Three whole steps, one half step	Melodic—stable, firm; harmonic—similar effect of stability
Augmented fifth	Four whole steps	Melodic and harmonic—unstable yet without clash
Minor sixth	Three whole steps, two half steps	Melodic—wide, yet relatively comfortable leap; harmonic—euphonious, blended quality
Major sixth	Four whole steps, one half step	Melodic and harmonic effects similar to those of minor sixth
Augmented sixth	Five whole steps	Harmonic—unsteady, tense
Minor seventh	Four whole steps, two half steps	Melodic—wide, unsteady leap; harmonic—unstable, somewhat edgy
Major seventh	Five whole steps, one half step	Melodic and harmonic effects similar to those of minor seventh, but with greater clash
Diminished seventh	Three whole steps, three half steps	Melodic—wide, unstable, yet tense in effect; harmonic—unstable, tense
Octave	Five whole steps, two half steps	Melodic and harmonic effects of firmness, openness, and stability

EXERCISES

1. Select a tone, sing various intervals, above and below, together and in succession.

2. Write down intervals as played or sung (aural recognition).

Sample intervals for Exercises 1 and 2

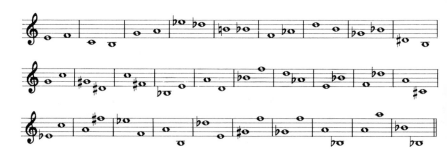

3. Analyze various melodic passages for concentration or emphasis upon various types of intervals. Relate the interval structure of the passages to the general character of the music.

Examples of analyses for Exercise 3

Brahms: Symphony No. 1, first movement, measures 130–142—diminished fifths and perfect fourths; a highly involuted melody

Smetana: Overture to *The Bartered Bride,* measures 8–31—major and minor seconds; rushing, yet smooth quality

Beethoven: Violin Concerto, finale—perfect fourths and thirds; neatly squared tune

Chapter Two

The Sense of Key

In Chap. 1 we noted that some intervals gave impressions of firmness and stability while other intervals conveyed a feeling of unsteadiness or instability. Running down the list we can sort out the harmonic intervals according to their degree of stability or instability:

Stable	*Relatively stable*	*Unstable*
Unison	Major, minor thirds	Sevenths
Octave	Major, minor sixths	Seconds
Perfect fifth		Augmented, diminished intervals

The perfect fourth appears as either stable or unstable according to position and use.

Stability and instability represent a means by which harmony may be related to musical action and structure through effects of musical movement and arrival. Musical sound acquires character and vitality when it moves forward in time. In turn, musical movement in time is controlled by points of arrival which set a goal, a resting point, or a point of articulation for the flow of sound. The interplay between movement and arrival is one of the fundamental aspects of the musical experience.

When we hear harmonic intervals in music which do not have a firmness or stability of effect, we sense the need for further action. Such intervals contribute to the effect of musical movement. When we hear intervals which seem firm and stable, we sense that the need for arrival or rest has been satisfied. In Ex. 1, the intervals marked "x" represent some quality of instability. Those marked "y" represent stability. Each contributes to the effects of movement or arrival.

EX. 1.   Instability and stability of intervals used for movement and arrival

a. Haydn: Sonata in E♭ major (1789–90), finale

18

b. Bartók: *Mikrokosmos,* Vol. VI, Subject and Reflection
Allegro

f ben ritmato

Copyright, 1940, by Hawkes and Son (London) Ltd. Reprinted by permission.

Each harmonic interval gives an impression of stability or instability in vary-ing degrees and to that extent may contribute to effects of movement or arrival in music. It is the ability of intervals to act in this manner that has made harmony such a powerful force in the shaping of musical structure throughout the history of Western music.

In the harmonic system of the eighteenth and nineteenth centuries, the system which underlies most of our familiar concert music, stability and instability of intervals have been coordinated into a comprehensive and logical plan. This plan is a practical working relationship between tones, and it is embodied for the listener in the *sense of key.*

Listen to the following examples:

EX. 2.   Key of C

a. Progression in the key of C

b. Scale of C

Example 2*a,* a series of harmonic intervals, centers upon and flows around the tone C, which we hear:

1. At the beginning.
2. From time to time throughout the example.
3. As a final point of arrival at the end.

Example 2*b* is a *scale,* a conjunct series of tones moving in one direction. This particular scale begins and ends on C. At the seventh tone B, we sense a strong expectation for the following C; this is so strong that we feel very much frustrated if we do not hear the C.

In both these examples the tones and intervals created a system of tones that enabled us to identify C as a point of arrival or reference. C was thus a *tonal center.* Both examples embodied a generally experienced effect which can be described as the *sense of key.* The sense of key in harmony depends upon interval relationships involving specific types of instability and sta-bility reacting upon each other. We shall now describe this creation of the sense of key in its clearest and most simple manifestation, the *major* key.

Example *2b* represents the scale of a major key. To Western ears, the major scale is one of the most familiar and convincing musical statements that can be made. This pattern, which we know so well and which we take so much for granted, has values and relationships within it that have tremendous significance for the harmonic procedures of centuries of Western music. We shall now look at some of these features.

1. *The major triad.* Play the note C; immediately add the notes E and G above it. Note that this combination strengthens the original impression of C. The upper notes add firmness in position and greater stability.

The sound of this three-note group, called the *major triad,* is one of the most perfectly satisfying impressions we can receive from music. Centuries ago, musical theorists gave it the name *armonia perfetta,* perfect harmony. (All major triads in the position given above consist of a major third above the lowermost tone and a perfect fifth as the outer interval.) Major triads epitomize the natural structure of a musical tone, that is, the *tone* itself and the tones of higher pitch that resonate as *partials* when a given tone is sung or played. This is called the harmonic series. Example 3 gives the harmonic series of C and shows how the first six tones represent an amplified major triad upon C.

EX. 3.　Major triad and harmonic series of C

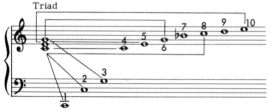

Sounded by itself, then, the major triad can give a firm and pleasant impression of a tonal center, an absolute effect of stability.

2. *The diatonic scale.* Using the white keys of the piano, play a scale upward from middle C to C an octave above. Do likewise with the tones D, E, F, etc. Then play the scales in Ex. *4b.*

EX. 4.　Diatonic and nondiatonic scales

a. Diatonic scales

b. Nondiatonic scales

Each of the scales in Ex. 4 has a distinctive character which arises from the special arrangement of half steps and whole steps. But the white-note scales have some qualities in common that distinguish them from the others given. These qualities are the following:

1. They are composed principally of whole steps, except for *two* half steps.
2. The two half steps are placed at the distance of a fourth or fifth from each other. This provides a *balanced* distribution of whole and half steps. This balance is reflected by the evenness and clarity of motion within such scales. (See Ex. 6, Chap. 1, which illustrates the differences in evenness and clarity between scales composed entirely of half steps or whole steps and a scale based upon the diatonic order.)

Thus, a scale is described in Western musical tradition as being *diatonic* when it is built of *five* whole steps among which are placed two half steps separated by the·distance of a fourth or fifth. The diatonic quality of the major scale is the second of its features which is important to its ability to define a tonal center, since from diatonicism it receives clarity and immediate intelligibility of organization.

3. *Position of the half steps and the tritone.* Various diatonic scales sound distinctive because of the position of the half steps among the eight tones. Half steps act as points of reference. When a melodic line reaches a half step, it "turns a corner"; half steps create a profile for a diatonic scale.

In Ex. 5, six scales are given. (In medieval and Renaissance times these were given names and designated as *modes*.) Note the positions of the half steps in each mode.

EX. 5.   Modal scales

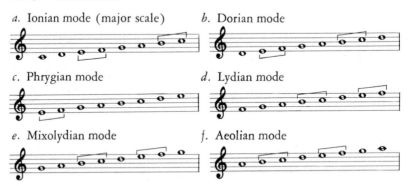

a. Ionian mode (major scale)   *b.* Dorian mode

c. Phrygian mode   *d.* Lydian mode

e. Mixolydian mode   *f.* Aeolian mode

Each of the above scales contains the *tritone* in the form of the augmented fourth or its inversion, the diminished fifth. *In music of the eighteenth and nineteenth centuries, whenever the tritone is heard, a need for its resolution is generated.* In this resolution *one* tone is accepted as the tonal center.

EX. 6.   Tritone moving to tonal center

a.   *b.*

In Ex. 6 we hear this strong value of tension of the tritone which needs to move forward to a point of resolution. A specific resolution is suggested. Such a resolution does appear following each of the intervals of tension in Ex. 6. The interval of resolution represents in each case the tonal center C. *In the major scale of C the resolution of the tritone affirms the impression of the tonal center.* However, when the tritone is resolved in the other diatonic scales, it does *not* affirm the tonal center, that is, the tone of departure and arrival, which is 1 or 8 of the scale.

The tritone is by far the most powerful agent of harmonic action or instability within our traditional harmonic system, exactly because it creates such an urgent need for resolution to a specific harmonic point. The major scale gains much of its strength from taking fullest advantage of the resolution tendencies of the tritone.

Three characteristics of the major scale, then, enable it to act as a firm, clear, convincing embodiment of a sense of key. These characteristics are the following:

1. Major triad as the representative of the tonal center (firm orientation)
2. Diatonic layout (smoothly organized relationships)
3. Tritone action leading to tonal center (convincing interaction between movement and arrival)

The most solid and emphatic embodiment of the sense of key is achieved in a section of music which does the following:

1. Begins with the *tonic* major triad (the triad of the tonal center)
2. Explores a bit, touching upon the tritone–to–tonal-center formula periodically
3. Ends firmly upon the tonic major triad, approaching it with a tritone effect

The following example demonstrates this embodiment of the sense of key:

EX. 7.   Embodiment of the key of C in a progression

Tonal centers may be represented by other than the major triad. Some systems of tone relationship and musical rhetoric have been evolved in the history of music that make lesser use of the major triad than the familiar tonal system does; for that matter, in some harmonic idioms the major triad is carefully avoided. Here are some examples of different types of tonal center:

EX. 8.   Minor triad as point of reference and arrival (see Chap. 3, page 26)

Johann Walter: *Aus tiefer Not* (sixteenth century)

EX. 9.   Single tone acting as a point of reference

Bartók: *Mikrokosmos,* Vol. VI, Free Variations (twentieth century)

Copyright, 1940, by Hawkes and Son (London) Ltd. Reprinted by permission.

EX. 10.   Perfect fifth acting as point of arrival and reference

Bartók: *Mikrokosmos,* Vol. II, Exercise

Copyright, 1940, by Hawkes and Son (London) Ltd. Reprinted by permission.

EX. 11.   Relatively stable combination of tones preceded by a more unstable combination creating a sense of relative repose

Hindemith: *Das Marienleben,* The Marriage at Cana (twentieth century)

Reprinted by permission of B. Schott's Soehne, Mainz, and Associated Music Publishers, Inc., New York, their United States representative.

(*Note:* The chord at "x" is considerably more unstable than the chord at "y,"
because of the diminished fifth *in the bass* in the former and the perfect fifth *in
the bass* in the latter. The interval set in the heavier, more massive area of sound
determines largely the quality of the combination.)

We can understand now, from the examples given in this chapter, that the tonal center represents something basic to musical meaning and organization. It functions in the following ways:

1. As a point of departure at the beginning
2. As a point of reference en route
3. As a point of arrival

Composers have arranged intervallic relationships in their music so as to give different impressions of tonal center. For our purpose, the system of the eighteenth and nineteenth centuries will be explored. This is the system based upon the major triad and its relationships.

In this chapter we have classified intervals as being stable or unstable. This distinction corresponds roughly to the conventional classification of *dissonant* and *consonant* intervals. No sharp line of demarcation separates these two categories. During the past one thousand years there have been many changing ideas as to what constitutes consonance and dissonance. The classification according to stability or instability has been made in order to show how consonance and dissonance values participate in projecting the impression of a tonal center and in creating harmonic action.

SUMMARY

1. The interplay of harmonic stability and instability contributes to musical movement and arrival and therefore to musical structure.

2. The major scale is the strongest embodiment of the sense of key, which organizes harmonic stability and instability in a specialized system.

3. The major scale embodies the sense of key because of the following characteristics:

a. The major triad as the representative of the key
b. The diatonic layout for evenness and balanced distribution of tones
c. The tritone in the 4–7 position, providing a strong drive to the tonal center

4. Other embodiments of tonal center include:

a. Minor triad
b. Single tone
c. Perfect fifth
d. Stability following instability

EXERCISES

1. In the following ten scales, determine by listening the position of the half steps (see pages 19 to 20).

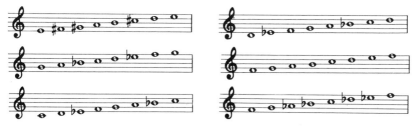

2. Determine, by listening and by visual analysis, which modal scales constitute the bases of the following melodies (see pages 20 to 21):

Chorale, *Aus tiefer Not*

Kyrie, Missa Cunctipotens

Schubert: Quintet in C major, Op. 163, finale

Allegretto

p

3. Determine, by listening, which of the following melodies are diatonic and which are chromatic (see page 19):

Stravinsky: *Le Sacre du printemps,* Part II

Copyright, 1921, by Edition Russe de Musique. Copyright assigned to Boosey & Hawkes, Inc., 1947. Reprinted by permission.

Purcell: *Dido and Aeneas,* Dido's Lament

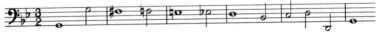

Brahms: Symphony No. 1, Op. 68, first movement

Allegro

p   dolce

Mozart: *Marriage of Figaro,* Non piu andrai

Allegro vivace

4. Listen to the following pieces to determine what impression of tonal center is given and in what manner (see pages 20 to 23):
a. Laus Deo Patri (plainsong)—departure and arrival upon the *tone* E

 b. *Drink to Me Only with Thine Eyes*—*major key* relationships
 c. Mendelssohn: *Hebrides* Overture (beginning)—*minor key*
 d. Bartók: *Mikrokosmos,* Vol. VI, Ostinato—*perfect fifth, single tone*
 e. Schönberg: *Pierrot lunaire* (first number)—*no* discernible tonal center
5. Select a given tone (for example, F) as a tonal center. Using accidentals, write various series of ten to twelve notes so that the passage will represent the following scales or systems:
 a. Phrygian
 b. Aeolian
 c. Dorian
 d. Mixolydian
 e. Lydian
 f. Two or three nondiatonic systems
Begin and end each passage on the selected tonal center.

Chapter Three

Triads; Voice Parts

We have dealt with single intervals in order to clarify questions of movement, arrival, and the creation of a sense of key. A musical passage most often contains more than a single harmonic interval heard at a given moment. To secure and amplify the sense of harmonic action and position for the listener, three, four, and perhaps more simultaneous tones are desirable; this is what we hear in a musical composition. In this way fullness and special qualities of sonority are created, values which are extremely important and which often give us the clue to the style and the expressive intent of a work.

The code by which fuller sound combinations were organized in Western music from 1400 to 1900 is called the *triad system*. If we reduce many of the fuller sounds in the music of Bach, Haydn, Schubert, Mendelssohn, and their contemporaries to the simplest components, we discover three different tones that line up exactly like, or similar to, the major triad.

In the following list, the traditional triads are described and illustrated:

1. *Major triad*. (See Chap. 2.)
2. *Minor triad*. Minor third, perfect fifth above the lowermost tone. Major third between two upper tones. The sound of the minor triad is not as bright and assertive as that of the major triad. This parallels the contrast between the major and minor thirds we described in Chap. 1.

The minor triad can be used to represent a tonal center. In the key-oriented harmony of the period 1700 to 1900, the minor triad became a full partner to the major as a tonal center by borrowing the 4–7 tritone. This was done by raising the seventh degree of the minor scale. Since the minor triad is less assertive than the major, compositions based upon a minor key frequently concluded with the major triad upon the tonic note. This was not done to convey an impression of a brighter mood but rather to secure the strongest effect of final arrival, to conclude as positively and firmly as possible.

EX 1.. Minor triad

3. *Diminished triad*. Minor third, diminished fifth above the lowermost note; minor third between two upper tones. Because of the presence of the diminished

fifth in the chord, you hear a compact, tight, unstable sound which creates a strong demand for resolution. The chord and its position in a progression are illustrated in Ex. 2.

EX. 2.   Diminished triad

4. *Augmented triad.* Augmented fifth, major third above the lowermost note. Major third between two upper tones. For the present we shall merely take note of this chord. It has a special value of color which later nineteenth-century composers found very attractive. When we take up coloristic harmony, we shall return to this chord.

EX. 3.   Augmented triad

CHORD POSITIONS

As the triads described above are used in musical compositions, their component tones appear in various vertical arrangements. These arrangements are classified according to which tone appears in the lowermost voice. When the *root* is in the bass, the chord is said to be in *root* position; *root* position is the most stable of all chord positions. When the *third* of the chord is in the lowermost voice, the chord is said to be in *first* inversion, which produces a less stable sound than does root position. When the *fifth* of the chord appears in the lowermost voice, the designation is *second* inversion, which is the least stable position of a triad. In the seventeenth and eighteenth centuries chord positions such as these and others were reckoned by interval from the lowermost voice. Thus, a triad in root position, which has a third and fifth above the root, received the signature $\frac{5}{3}$; similarly, first inversions were indicated by $\frac{6}{3}$; second inversions by $\frac{6}{4}$.

EX. 4.   Positions of triads

a. Root position *b.* First inversion *c.* Second inversion

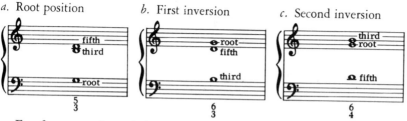

For five centuries, triads have represented the basic sound of Western harmony. Until about 1400, fourths and fifths made up the pervading sound of medieval music. Since 1900, composers have worked increasingly with nontriadic combinations, partly in order to try new sonority effects, partly because the vigor and clarity of melodic and rhythmic action became greater with combinations that did not blend well. The major triad, the prototype of all triad forms, presents a compact, sweet, blended sound; it is an ideal vehicle both for projection of attractive sonority values and for the embodiment of a tonal center.

VOICE PARTS

A full sound or texture generally includes from three to five, six, or more tones, covering the range of sound from high to low. Some instruments, such as the piano, harp, and organ, can negotiate the full range of musical sound. Other instruments and the human voice cover but a segment of the total range.

Traditionally, voices and instruments have been ranged in four groups:

1. Soprano (the highest)
2. Alto (medium high)
3. Tenor (middle or medium low)
4. Bass (lowermost)

There is no fixed limit for the individual ranges; they overlap to a great extent, as Ex. 5 illustrates:

EX. 5.   Part ranges

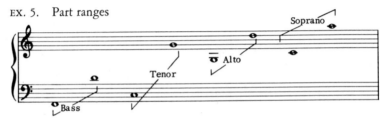

Musical instruments, even those of limited range, possess ranges which generally extend over several (two or three) of the standard vocal ranges. Nevertheless, when several voices are performing together, each assumes a role (soprano, alto, tenor, bass) in a range that will have a specific relation to the total texture, as in Ex. 6.

EX. 6.   Roles played by different voices

Mozart: Quartet in C major, K. 465, first movement

When a composer is setting a composition in full texture, he must give consideration to other aspects of voice relationships, such as:

1. *Doubling.* When three separate tones are available in a triad and four, five, six, or more voices are performing, certain tones must be duplicated, or *doubled,* generally at different octaves. The manner in which a composer doubles the tones will affect the color of the chord. As a rule, in major and minor triads the *root,* or lowermost tone, receives preference, because it imparts stability and firmness to the sound of the chord. Doubling the third or fifth gives a somewhat different effect, very desirable or even necessary in some cases. Here are some examples of doubling (see also Chap. 8).

EX. 7.   Doubling

a. Root doubled   *b.* Third doubled   *c.* Fifth doubled

d. Third doubled; fifth doubled

Mendelssohn: *Song without Words,* Op. 19, no. 8

2. *Spacing.* Spacing refers to the distance between the various tones of a chord. *Close* position designates a compact arrangement of the tones in which the voices above the bass are as close to each other as possible; it also refers to chords in which the entire compass, from bass to soprano, does not

exceed an octave and a fifth. *Open* position refers to a wider spread among the tones.

As you can very easily hear, the effect of the spacing of a chord bears strongly upon its expressive quality. When composers are scoring, they pay particular attention to spacing, which achieves for them the final effect of color proper to the style and manner of their music. As a rule, close position gives the effect of firmness, compactness, and a close blend; open positions lend themselves to special effects of sonority.

EX. 8.   Spacing

a. Close positions   *b.* Open positions

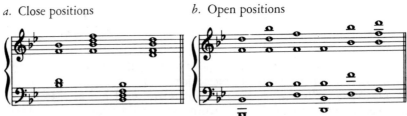

As you can hear, the position within the total range at which individual tones are placed also has a strong bearing upon the color value. Extreme ranges have very striking effects; the middle range, in contrast, has a more neutral and well-balanced effect.

The composer also is concerned with the type of instrument to which he assigns different tones. The color of a chord can be shaded very much according to the tone qualities of the instruments performing the sound. However, this is a matter for instrumentation and will only concern us if we set some of our projects for instruments.

In the past three centuries of Western music, by far the most important voices in texture have been the outer voices, the principal melodic voice (soprano) and the foundation voice (bass), which provides the major support to the musical action.

EX. 9.   Action of outer voices

Beethoven: Sonata in C minor, Op. 13, second movement

The relationship in Ex. 9 can be described as a *polarity* of outer voices. Since the seventeenth century this polarity has been the textural framework of most musical composition. Often we can strip a typical passage down to its melody and its bass and still retain the essential features of the musical action.

We too shall begin writing music in two parts, an upper part and a supporting lower part. This approach differs from the usual method of teaching harmony, which begins with writing of four-part chord progressions. We have mentioned briefly some of the advantages of this approach (see Preface). More specifically, these advantages are as follows:

1. We deal with a small amount of material which we can handle flexibly; thus we can reach for something that has immediate musical value. In two-part writing we need not be concerned with marshaling four voices into some kind of errorless order, a problem that would ordinarily occupy our entire time and attention.

2. Since, in two parts, both the music and the work move more quickly than in four-part writing, a phrase can take shape very quickly. Thus we can come directly to grips with the problems of key definition and rhythmic structure. When we deal with full chords, we must make decisions regarding sonority, spacing, doubling, harmonic color, voice leading; in the beginning stages of our study this would put the brake upon musical action and the growth of musical structure.

3. In two-part writing we can combine procedures; there is room for melodic and rhythmic elaboration; later, texture can be developed and expanded. Thus, we can cover more ground, gaining an understanding of phrase structure and periods.

4. This approach encourages creative activity from the very beginning.

5. The essential aspects of this approach—(*a*) emphasis on the voices which carry the principal responsibility for action, (*b*) concern with techniques of key definition, (*c*) the manipulation of characteristic, idiomatic harmonic, rhythmic, and melodic formulas—all provide the terms of a technique of analysis which gives us insight into the style and structure of great works of musical art.

EXERCISES

1. Identify the following triads by listening; indicate the kind of triad and its position (see pages 26 to 27):

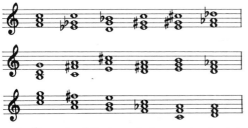

2. On each of the tones below, write the following triads (see pages 26 to 27):

a. Major $\frac{5}{3}$ *f.* Major $\frac{6}{4}$

b. Minor $\frac{6}{4}$ *g.* Diminished $\frac{5}{3}$

c. Diminished $\frac{6}{3}$ *h.* Major $\frac{6}{3}$

d. Augmented $\frac{6}{3}$ *i.* Minor $\frac{6}{3}$

e. Minor $\frac{5}{3}$ *j.* Diminished $\frac{6}{4}$

Sing each triad.

3. Discover in music literature various types of triads (see pages 26 to 27).

Sample for Exercise 3

Mozart: Sonata in E♭ major, K. 282, first movement

4. In a given passage analyze the doubling and spacing of triads (see pages 29 to 30).

Sample for Exercise 4

Beethoven: Sonata in B♭ major, Op. 22, second movement

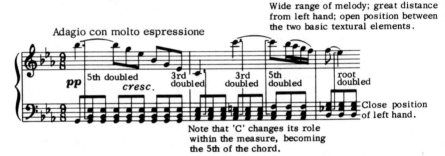

5. Reduce the following passages from music literature to the two polar voices, soprano and bass (see pages 30 to 31):

Brahms: Requiem, *Ye That Are Now Sorrowful*

Beethoven: Sonata in E♭, Op. 81*a*, first movement

Schumann: *Three Piano Sonatas for Young People,* Op. 118, Second Sonata, Evening Song

Part Two

Harmonic Action

Chapter Four

The Cadential Formula

The harmonic relationships we have studied thus far—intervals, the sense of key, stability and instability, triads—these have enormous potential for harmonic action. Indeed, it is the power to carry musical movement forward and at the same time to control and focus movement that gives harmony its importance in the structure of eighteenth- and nineteenth-century music. The ensuing part of our study will be devoted to the ways in which harmony relates to musical structure through harmonic action and the sense of harmonic position.

We pointed out in Chap. 2 that harmonic action, like all action, proceeds through a cycle of *departure, movement,* and *arrival.* A phase of movement is thus created, directed to a point of arrival. Each point of arrival becomes, in turn, a new point of departure; so, musical structure takes shape by a series of phases of movement. This action was illustrated in Exs. 6 and 7 of Chap. 2.

In eighteenth- and nineteenth-century music the harmonic embodiment of this cycle was realized by a number of characteristic patterns and formulas. Certainly the most important of these by far was what we shall here designate as the *cadential formula.*

Generally, the cadential formula involves two basic aspects of harmony:

1. Instability, as represented by the tritone
2. Stability, as represented by harmony of the tonal center

Steps 4 and 7 of the major scale provide us with the *movement-instability* factor of the cadential formula; this must be followed by step 1, which represents *arrival-stability.* When the cycle of 4–7 to 1 is completed, a clear sense of key is created, and a *small segment of musical structure has taken shape.* The interdependence of movement and arrival factors enables us to construct musical syntax very much as groups of words are linked together to create meaning in language.

No one yet has explained satisfactorily the acoustical or physiological basis of the 4–7–1 cycle, but we do know that, from a practical standpoint, it has been critically important as a cohesive force throughout the past five centuries of Western music. It is exemplified in the music of Bach, Handel, Mozart, Haydn, Beethoven, Schubert, Brahms, Wagner, and many other composers. It fairly saturates their musical language, constantly renewing and refreshing itself through varieties of texture, position, and structure. It provides for us a guide to organizing tone relationships, to voice leading, and even to sonority values. It is the one common denominator for music of this era. Moreover, it is easy to grasp, manipulate, and understand, because its aural effect is so clear and commanding. Therefore, we begin our study of harmony itself by investigating the cadential formula.

For purposes of identification we shall give traditional names to the cadential tones:

1   is designated as being *tonic* in function.
4   is designated as being *subdominant* in function.
7   is designated as being *dominant,* or *leading-tone,* in function.

In the order of their action, as we observe in musical literature:

1   appears as a point of *departure.*
4   represents *digression.*
7   turns the corner and *points to home.*
1   is *home* again, the point of *arrival.*

This is how the progression looks melodically:

EX. 1.   Melodic cadential formula

Following is an example with harmonic treatment of the cadential formula:

EX. 2.   Harmonic cadential formula

The two voices share the essential tones.

Observe how movement and arrival can be maintained by overlapping points of arrival with points of departure in successive cadential formulas. A more extended harmonic flow is thus created.

EX. 3.   Series of cadential formulas

* When brackets are used in subsequent examples as follows: ⌐1 4 7 1 4 7 1⌐, they describe cadential formulas.

In the flow of harmonic movement the proper order of the cadential formula is 1–4–7–1. Yet these degrees are strongly bound up with each other in the definition of a key; they have such strong attraction to each other that whenever they are sounded in close proximity, they will project the cadential effect and define the key. Thus, in the following progression we have 1–7–4–3; nevertheless, we still hear 1 as the tonal center, the point of reference.

EX. 4. 1–7–4–3 cadential formula

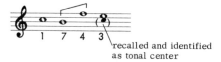

1   7   4   3
recalled and identified
as tonal center

Later in this chapter other variants of the cadential formula will be described.

Here are some excerpts from eighteenth-century musical literature which are built around 1–4–7–1 cadential formulas. The tones in heavy print represent 1, 4, and 7.

EX. 5. 1–4–7–1 cadential formulas

a. Bach, J. S.: Partita in E minor from *The Little Notebook*

b. Beethoven: Quartet in A major, Op. 18, no. 5, first movement

c. Mozart: Quartet in E♭ major, K. 428

In the two-part sketches above (Exs. 2 and 3) various tones were combined effectively with 1, 4, and 7. The intervals created might be considered to be segments of triads, since later on we shall add a third tone to amplify the sound, creating full triads. These triads will then take part, just as our present intervals do, in the action of the cadential formula.

For the present, we shall list the preferable two-part combinations:

1 combines well with itself (octave, unison), 3, and 5 (provided 5 stands *above* 1 in range; otherwise, the unstable interval of the perfect fourth is created unsatisfactory for our purposes). 6 is sometimes used with 1.

4 combines well with 6, 2, itself, and 1 (provided 1 stands *above* 4).

7 combines well with 5, 4, and 2.

These intervals are illustrated in Ex. 6 in a variety of positions.

EX. 6. Intervals for cadential formulas

a. Combinations with 1

occasionally

b. Combinations with 4

c. Combinations with 7

You will note that in no case is the perfect fourth used as an interval in our two-part formulas. When the lower note of the perfect fourth sounds as the lowermost note of a chord or interval, an effect of instability is created. Unless this effect of instability is handled in certain typical ways, it does not fit in with the system of cadential harmony we are exploring. Later, we shall demonstrate how this effect can be employed in a very telling structural manner. For the present, we shall bypass the perfect fourth.

At present we shall not compose with full triads. Yet we can obtain a clearer perspective of chord formation by listing the triads of a key, with their commonly assigned names. Example 7 shows the way in which the

EX. 7. Triads in the key of C major (compare with Ex. 6)

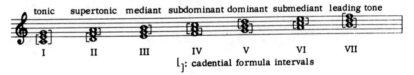

tonic	supertonic	mediant	subdominant	dominant	submediant	leading tone
I	II	III	IV	V	VI	VII

⌊⌉: cadential formula intervals

intervals which are available in the cadential formula fit into various triads.

We shall describe intervals according to their function in the cadential formula, that is, 1, 4, or 7. In addition we shall indicate by Roman numeral which triads contain the intervals.

ADDITIONAL CADENTIAL FORMULAS

If you examine the cadential progressions in eighteenth-century music, you often find that the 1–4–7–1 does not always appear consecutively. Often 1–7–1 is used at the beginning of a passage; we also find 1–$\frac{4}{7}$–1 when the tritone is used. Occasionally we discover 1–4–1. Frequently, harmony of a given function may be restated at a different position. Below we have some examples of these procedures:

EX. 8. Variants of the basic cadential formula

When we use the cadential formulas described in this chapter we create a strong and pervasive feeling of key. This key feeling is so much in evidence that we may occasionally use intervals to represent subdominant or dominant harmony that lack the 1, 4, or 7. In such cases, the cadential action is not weakened for two reasons:

1. We have a strong and immediate impression of 1, 4, or 7 in other cadential formulas in the piece.
2. The interval in question suggests, or outlines, a chord which, were it set in three or four voices, would contain the 4 or 7.

EX. 9. Cadential formulas lacking 1, 4, or 7

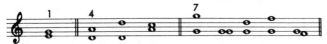

f.

g. Intervals lacking 1, 4, or 7

The chords implied or suggested by each interval in the cadential formulas in Ex. 9 were indicated by their proper Roman numeral. This procedure is advisable because it helps to develop both familiarity with the triads of a key and flexibility in their use. As you work, it is well to keep in mind which chords represent specific cadential functions:

Tonic	Subdominant	Dominant
I.	IV	V
VI	II	VII

Although III contains the leading tone, it uses it as part of a completely stable interval, the perfect fifth. Therefore, it lacks the sense of movement within the key which is necessary to create the dominant function of a satisfactory cadence.

Among the cadential formulas we have been studying it is quite apparent that a considerable difference exists with respect to their strength and their ability to convey a sense of arrival. In tonic harmony, the sturdier effect of arrival occurs when the tonic note is in the lower part. This corresponds to a root position in the tonic triad. When such an interval is preceded by dominant harmony in which the lower note is the fifth of the scale, an extremely strong effect of arrival is achieved. Such a progression is admirably suited to bring a passage to a satisfactory close. At other times, it may halt movement and therefore have an undesirable effect. Hence, it is recommended that the 5–1 cadential formula action in the lower voice be reserved for the final formula. This progression is called the *authentic cadence.*

EX. 10.   Series of cadential formulas ending with authentic cadence

It is also possible to arrive at the end of a musical passage without giving the impression of a final close. One very familiar method of accomplishing such an effect of arrival is by means of the *half cadence.* This calls for a stop upon dominant harmony, generally with the fifth degree of the key in the lowermost voice.

EX. 11. Cadential formulas ending with half cadences

The half cadence leaves something to be said further. We may continue with more cadential formulas, but until we reach an authentic cadence, a clear and emphatic sense of completion is lacking.

EX. 12. Relationship between half and authentic cadences

The sections marked off by the successive cadences would form the harmonic bases in length and in action for musical *phrases;* the entire passage, from beginning to end, with arrival at an authentic cadence, constitutes a musical *period.* In later chapters the composition of phrases and periods will be explained in relation to rhythmic and melodic materials.

VOICE LEADING

The tone relationships we have been exploring—interval sounds, the sense of key, the cadential formula—these may all be likened to *chemical* affinities between tones. Tones are like elements which connect with each other to form simple or elaborate compounds, such as intervals, chords, and keys. When this was done we felt an inner coherence, character, and logic in the new structure, something analogous to what a crystal might show in a chemical substance.

There is another technique for establishment of coherence in musical progression. That is the movement of one tone to another in a melodic progression. Indeed, this is a much more pervasive and far older procedure than the tonal relationships of intervals and keys. It may be regarded as a *mechanical* method of achieving continuity and coherence. We can illustrate its effect as follows:

EX. 13. Cohesive effect of melodic movement

44

In the scale of C given above we can easily sense the melodic direction. It is smooth, clear, and thoroughly predictable. It makes good musical sense, gathering all its tones into a clearly projected pattern. If we take the same tones and rearrange them so that disjunct movement pervades, the result has much less coherence, although it might be much more interesting. Melodic movement must achieve, thus, a balance between coherence and distinctive action.

As a rule, conjunct movement provides connection, disjunct movement heightens interest. In medieval plainsong, the ideal of expression was a smooth, gently fluctuating quality of movement; hence, the melodic lines of plainsong are principally conjunct, with a quiet rise and fall of the melodic line. In much contemporary music, the ideal of expression is a violent, dramatically compact quality of movement; hence, the melodic lines highlight wide leaps, abrupt and frequent changes of direction, with few conjunct passages.

For our present purposes, we rely on conjunct movement. The two factors which will provide us with musical coherence, the cadential formula and conjunct melodic movement, give a maximum of binding action and permit us to move forward smoothly and quickly. We welcome disjunct movement but only as it is held in check and compensated for by conjunct movement. In the following example, note how the smooth action of the component voices binds the progression together convincingly.

EX. 14.   Conjunct melodic movement

Mozart: Quartet in C major, K. 465, finale

When voices are moving together, a composite pattern of melodic action is created. Each voice has its own outline that is set against the melodic outline of other voices. This play of outlines and patterns is an important aspect of musical composition. When melodic lines move simultaneously, their relationship has two aspects:

1. The directions in which they move, that is, *counterdirection*
2. The points in time at which they move, that is, *countertime*

When we begin to use rhythmic elaboration, we shall deal with counter-time. Now, we should become conversant with types of counterdirection. These are illustrated below:

EX. 15. Types of counterdirection in melodic movement

Below are examples of various types of melodic movement taken from musical literature.

EX. 16. Melodic movement

Mozart: Quartet in C major, K. 465, first movement

Mozart: Quartet in C major, K. 465, first movement

(*continued*)

PARALLEL FIFTHS AND OCTAVES

Ever since the fifteenth century the movement of a pair of voices in parallel fifths or octaves has been considered objectionable in sound, since the effect is somewhat inconsistent with counterline procedure and with the flexible play of interval sonorities. This is not to say that parallel fifths and octaves have not been written and used effectively; in some cases, their special effect is exactly what has been desired by the composer. However, in the exposed two-voice writing of your present work, apparent parallel fifths and octaves do not fit in well. Consider the following example:

EX. 17.   Parallel fifths and octaves

At "x" and "y" we sense a disturbing element, a harmonic effect that is not assimilated into the general idiom. These are parallel fifths and octaves. We can improve the effect by the following means:

EX. 18.   Correction of parallel fifths and octaves of Ex. 17.

If you arrive at an octave or fifth between the two voices, you will be in trouble if the interval immediately preceding is the same interval; if the octave or fifth at which you arrive is on a stressed rhythmic point, it should not be preceded by the same interval on a stressed point in the preceding measure. Here we have some examples:

EX. 19.   Rhythmic positions of parallel octaves and fifths

In two voices, corrections are easily made.

SUMMARY

1. 1–4–7–1 creates a cycle of stability and instability that defines a key. This cycle is called the basic cadential formula.

2. The interaction of the tones of the cadential formula is present whether the intervals employed are melodic or harmonic.

3. Cadential formulas may be linked together to create a series of cadential cycles.

4. Cadential action is supported when other tones are combined with tones of the cadential formula. These additional tones are:

1 combined with 3, 5, or 6
4 combined with 2, 6, or 1
7 combined with 2, 4, or 5

5. Occasionally 1, 4, or 7 may not be present in a cadential formula; yet, cadential action proceeds, since the essential tone is then implied.

6. The triads of a key are named according to the root tone. These are: I, tonic; II, supertonic; III, mediant; IV, subdominant; V, dominant; VI, submediant; VII, leading tone. Intervals which comprise cadential formulas may be thought of as incomplete triads. Complete triads will then further reinforce cadential action.

7. The strongest cadential formula, in which 5 moves to 1 in the lowermost voice, is called the authentic cadence. It is reserved for strong points of arrival.

8. A stop upon 7 or implied-7 harmony provides a half cadence effect.

9. Conjunct motion is preferable for smooth melodic action as cadential formulas and longer progressions are being written. Two tones may move in parallel, oblique, similar or contrary movement. Parallel movement at the distance of a perfect fifth or octave is not consistent with the styles being studied.

EXERCISES

1. Write the following two-part cadential formulas from dictation. Indicate the function of each interval by the Arabic numeral 1, 4, or 7 (see pages 37 to 42).

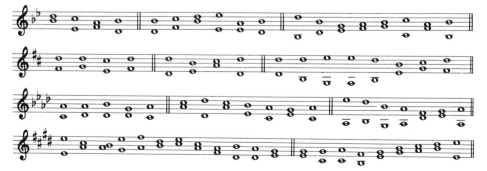

2. Reduce the following passages from musical literature to their basic cadential formulas (see page 39).

Samples for Exercise 2

Haydn: *Symphonie concertante,* Op. 84, first movement

Mozart: Sonata in C major, K. 279, first movement

Beethoven: Sonata in A major, Op. 2, no. 2, first movement, measures 1–9
Chopin: Rondo, Op. 1, piu lento section, measures 1–4
Schubert: Sonata in E♭, Op. 122, Menuetto, measures 1–8
Haydn: Sonata in G major (1766), first movement, measures 1 and 2
Bach: *Well-Tempered Clavier,* Book I, Prelude in C major, measures 1–4
Mendelssohn: *Song without Words,* Op. 53, no. 2, measures 1–5
Schumann: *Three Piano Sonatas for Young People,* Op. 118, Second Sonata, first movement, measures 1–5

3. Add upper or lower voice as indicated to complete two-voice cadential formulas. State function of each interval, bracket the formulas, indicate by Roman numeral below the triad in which the interval is contained. (See page 38.)

Add lower part

Add upper part

4. Compose two-voice cadential formulas. Include variants such as *changes in position* during a single function, *implications* of 1, 4, and 7, *omission* of 4 or 7 stage (see pages 38–39, 41–42).

Chapter Five

The Minor Mode

Our work to this point has been with the major mode. Major harmony represents the basis of traditional harmonic practice. For three centuries, and at the present time, it has been and remains the principal harmonic force. New harmonic systems have been devised recently; experiments with many different varieties of tone relationship have been made; yet, most of the music with which we come into contact shows direct influence, in its harmony, of the major mode.

This influence has extended to other scales and systems. In particular, it has made the *minor* mode a virtual partner in the key-centered harmonic system of Western music. In order to explain how this comes about, we shall recapitulate from Chap. 2.

The three elements of the major mode that enabled it to embody a key sense so well were:

1. The major triad
2. Diatonic layout
3. The position of the tritone

Example 1 gives the *natural* minor scale.

EX. 1. Natural minor scale

Of the three qualities listed above, this scale has but one, namely, *diatonic* layout. This makes for an even, coherent impression. The natural minor scale lacks the major triad as a tonic, yet it possesses within its tonic triad the *perfect fifth,* the essential ingredient of stability in a triad. Therefore, the minor triad could stand as a point of arrival and as a tonal center. But this scale lacks totally the action of the tritone between 4 and 7 which demands resolution to the tonic. The tritone of the minor scale stands between 2 and 6.

However, we can borrow the tritone action of the major mode by raising the seventh degree of the minor mode. Listen to the following example:

EX. 2. Minor mode with raised seventh degree (harmonic)

There is no question that we must move forward to 8 as we reach 7 in Ex. 2. With such a leading tone the minor mode has the essential ingredients for cadential key definition, that is, 4, 7, and 1 exactly as they appear in the major mode. In addition, the stability factor of 1 and 5 is present. To illustrate the difference in effect, here are two harmonizations of the same phrase, one using the *natural* minor mode, the other using the minor mode with leading tone, designated as the *harmonic* minor mode.

EX. 3. Two versions of phrase in minor mode

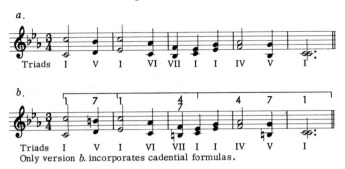

Only version *b.* incorporates cadential formulas.

As you can hear, the natural minor has a soft, somewhat plaintive quality which is in contrast to the greater assertive effect of the harmonic minor. Here, we place emphasis upon the action aspect of harmony rather than upon its special color values. Hence, we shall deal principally with the harmonic minor mode.

In the harmonic minor, the diatonic feeling may be disturbed by the augmented second created between 6 and 7 when a leading tone is provided. This disturbance applies particularly to vocal music, since the augmented second is a rather awkward interval to sing. To accommodate smoothness of melodic action it is possible to raise the sixth degree temporarily at the point required, not necessarily elsewhere in the piece. For purposes of classification, the scale that results is designated as the *melodic* minor. It is illustrated below:

EX. 4. Melodic minor scale

Often as not, in instrumental music of the eighteenth and nineteenth centuries, composers have preferred to retain the augmented second in melodic movement between 6 and 7; the interval imparts some greater expressive intensity to a melodic line.

Example 5 shows passages from musical literature in the minor mode, reduced to their underlying cadential formulas.

EX. 5. Reductions of minor mode passages to cadential formulas

a. Mozart: Sonata in D major, K. 284, finale, Var. VII

b. Bach: Two-part Invention in B minor

In Ex. 6 two-voice cadential formulas in the minor mode are illustrated. These employ either the minor or the major sixth degree. Note that some of the examples below use both versions of the sixth degree.

EX. 6. Cadential formulas in the minor mode

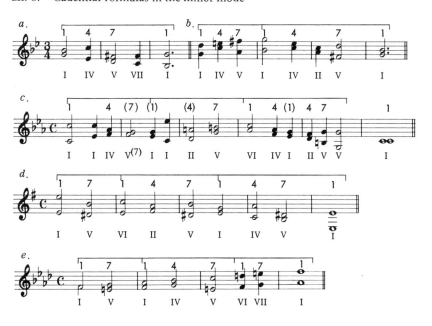

Although the minor mode, by virtue of its borrowed leading tone, has virtually the same structural strength as the major mode, its particular appeal lies in its rich palette of colors. As its two variable tones, the sixth and seventh degrees, are incorporated into various harmonies, they can create striking nuances, intermingling major and minor in a rich chiaroscuro. In a later chapter we shall investigate some of the special attributes of the minor mode.

SUMMARY

1. In order to function as a key, the minor mode must be furnished with a tritone between 4 and 7. Therefore, 7 is raised to create the harmonic minor mode.

2. In order to provide smooth upward movement between 6 and 7, avoiding the augmented second, the sixth degree may be raised temporarily, creating the melodic minor mode.

3. In all its basic structural functions, its cadential formulas, and its cadences, the minor mode behaves in the same manner as the major mode. Its color values are more striking because of the intermingling of major and minor through the raising of the seventh degree.

EXERCISES

1. Reduce the following passages to their basic cadential formulas (see page 51 and Chap. 4, page 39):

Bach: Two-part Invention in F minor, measures 1–4

Schumann: *Three Piano Sonatas for Young People,* Op. 118, Third Sonata, Gypsy Dance measures 1–8

Mendelssohn: *Song without Words,* Op. 53, no 5, measures 1–6

Haydn: Sonata in B minor (1776), first movement, measures 1–8

Chopin: Étude, Op. 25, no. 4, measures 1–5

Beethoven: String Quartet in C minor, Op. 18, no. 4, first movement, measures 1–8

2. Write the following cadential formulas from dictation. List the function and the implied triad (see page 51).

3. Add a lower or upper voice as indicated to the given lines to create cadential formulas in the minor mode (see page 51).

Add lower voice

Add upper voice

4. Write a number of cadential formulas in the minor mode according to the following directions (see pages 50 to 51):

  a. 1–4–7–1 ; 1–4–7–1 using raised sixth degree
  b. Formulas without 4 or 7
  c. Series of interlocking formulas, ending with the authentic cadence

Chapter Six

Rhythmic Elaboration: The Phrase

The 1–4–7–1 cycle of the cadential formula gives us a basic kind of harmonic logic—as it were, good musical grammar. Cadential formulas lend themselves to elaboration, since they provide solid frameworks as a start.

From this point we shall begin to explore the possibilities for elaborating cadential formulas. With each type of elaboration we shall find that our exercises will acquire expressive content.

The elaborations are of the following kinds:

1. Rhythmic elaboration—characteristic rhythmic patterns
2. Melodic elaboration—distinctive melodic patterns
3. Textural elaboration—sonority values and part writing
4. Harmonic elaboration—expansion of chord vocabulary and key relationships
5. Structural elaboration—combination of cadential formulas into complete musical statements

RHYTHMIC ELABORATION

When a single tone is broken up rhythmically or melodically, a certain amount of musical movement is released. This is analogous to the release of chemical, electric, or heat energy as a physical substance is broken up.

For example, we receive but one musical impression from a whole note that may extend through two or three seconds of time. As we listen to such a tone, our attention is strongest probably at the instant the tone is sounded; the impact of the tone starts musical movement. After this impact our interest and attention will dwindle somewhat; nothing new is added, and the whole note "coasts" by previously established momentum to its last instant.

On the other hand, if we break up this same whole note into various rhythmic patterns, we create a series of impressions, or impacts, which sustain and perhaps increase our attention and interest. Example 1 illustrates this process.

EX. 1. Rhythmic elaboration of whole note

This is a process of *rhythmic elaboration,* a process which composers have used for hundreds of years to give freshness and new momentum to the basic harmonic and melodic patterns of music. This breaking up of longer tones creates *rhythmic motives;* these are distinctive patterns which carry forward musical movement.

Rhythmic elaboration can become very complex; a great many notes can fill the given time interval. More generally, it remains quite simple, with sufficient activity only to give a characteristic style and quality of movement. Excessive elaboration defeats the purpose of momentum; it slows down the pace.

Many of the most useful rhythmic patterns in musical composition have been evolved originally in connection with dancing; dance music has been an extremely fertile source of motives for musical composition. Below we list some characteristic dance patterns:

EX. 2. Characteristic rhythmic patterns of dances

a. Waltz
Quickly

b. Habanera (also tango)
Rather slow

c. Polonaise
Moderately

d. Minuet (late eighteenth century)
Rather fast

e. Gavotte

Moderately

f. Bourrée (contredanse)

Quickly

In Ex. 3 the rhythmic patterns of a number of melodies are given. (Each bracket represents a single cadential formula.)

EX. 3.   Rhythmic patterns of melodies

a. Mendelssohn: *Songs without Words,* Op. 62, no. 4

b. Mozart: Sonata in B♭, K. 570, finale

c. Haydn: Symphony in C minor, Menuetto

RHYTHMIC MOTIVES AND THEIR RELATIONSHIPS

A rhythmic motive is a minute musical statement; statements call for counterstatements. The relationship between a statement and its counterstatement creates balance, symmetry, or a sense of completion. This relationship is another extremely important method for creating musical coherence.

Counterstatements can have three general relationships to preceding statements:

1. Repetition
2. Variation
3. Contrast

In Ex. 4 we illustrate a single motive, answered in three different examples by repetition of the rhythmic pattern, variation of the rhythmic pattern, contrast by means of a decidedly different counterstatement:

EX. 4.   Various types of counterstatement

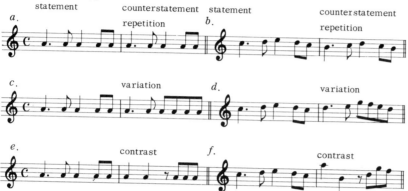

In a series of three, four, or more motives, two or three different relationships can be used effectively in alternation:

EX. 5.   Combinations of statement-counterstatement relationship

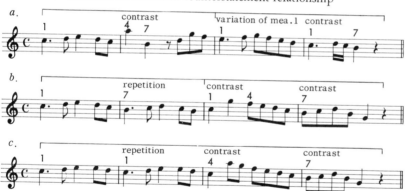

Generally speaking, strict repetition runs the danger of becoming monotonous. The ear welcomes change after an opening statement. On the other hand, too great a contrast may cause the music to sound somewhat disjointed or pieced together. Variation is always interesting and remains relatively easy for the listener to grasp; therefore, it is probably the most reliable way of spinning out a phase of musical movement in the rhythmic sense.

In the following example, we have taken a single cadential formula in two voices and have elaborated the upper voice rhythmically. The motive relationships are indicated.

EX. 6. Rhythmic elaboration of upper voice

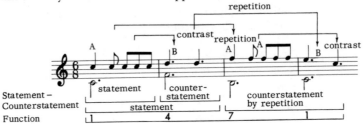

In Ex. 7, the rhythmic motive relationships in various melodies are analyzed.

EX. 7. Relationships of rhythmic motives

a. Beethoven: Sonata in E♭, Op. 31, no. 3, Menuetto

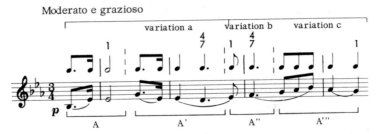

b. Schubert: Sonata, Op. 122, Menuetto

c. Haydn: Sonata in A♭ major, finale

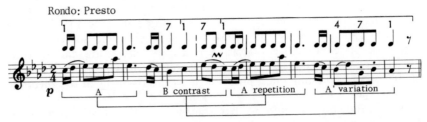

Both voices can participate in the rhythmic elaboration. Together they can make a composite pattern which has considerable interest because of the action and counteraction of the two parts. In such an arrangement, each part has but a fraction of the responsibility for carrying rhythmic movement forward. Consequently, there is an ease of movement and an economy of action in each part, much more so than if one part were taking the total responsibility for rhythmic action. Below are some examples of composite rhythmic elaboration:

EX. 8.   Composite rhythmic elaboration

In Chap. 4 we mentioned the possibility of restating or extending the harmony of a given cadential function. If we apply rhythmic elaboration in such a case we may be able to set two or perhaps more rhythmic motives into one phase of the cadential formula, as follows:

EX. 9.   Several motives within one harmony

a. Mozart: *Marriage of Figaro,* Non piu andrai

b. Beethoven: Symphony No. 3, first movement

THE PHRASE

In the examples studied thus far, we have explored the following elements of structure:

1. The cycle of departure, movement, and arrival as embodied in the cadential formula
2. The relationship of statement and counterstatement by repetition, contrast, and variation as embodied in rhythmic motives
3. The creation of a distinct manner of expression by rhythmic motives in characteristic styles
4. The convincing point of arrival, that is, the cadence, which brings a musical passage to a close

When these elements work together in a passage extending over three to eight measures, a musical *phrase* is created. Thus, the illustrations in Exs. 3 to 9 qualify as phrases.

The musical phrase is analogous to a phrase or clause in language. Both in music and in language, phrases contain clearly formed ideas, yet lack something in form or sense to be complete musical structures. This is due to the brevity of the statement, or perhaps to the fact that its point of arrival, though strong and clear, may not serve to bring movement to a satisfactory state of rest. Specifically, we can define the phrase as follows:

1. It is readily understood as a unit; its rhythmic motives and melodic shape have clear relationships among themselves.
2. It contains a distinctive and well-formed musical idea; it conveys something definite in the way of musical expression.
3. It has a sense of progression to a point of arrival; its cadential formulas, rhythmic motives, melodic shapes point to some goal.

Phrases are the structural units of most of the music we know. Compositions are built up in a chain of phrases, each of which performs a function in carrying forward a definite plan of musical action. Careful attention to well-shaped, convincing phrase structure will help to bridge the gap that exists between the composer's general idea of his piece and the specific details of motivic and harmonic action.

In eighteenth- and nineteenth-century music, the standard, or "normal," length for the phrase was four measures. This reflects the tremendous influence of dance music during these style periods. While many phrases in music of this time were shorter or longer, nevertheless the four-measure phrase was taken to be the norm and was used as a point of reference in musical composition. Moreover, many phrases of greater length than four measures were predicated upon the four-measure plan. To the imaginative composer the four-measure phrase was not a vise which restricted his freedom; rather, he regarded it as a firm platform from which he could confidently launch his greater musical flights.

SUMMARY

1. The first step in elaboration is to break up tones of the cadential formula into distinctive rhythmic patterns.

2. These rhythmic patterns often embody familiar dance types.

3. These rhythmic patterns, i.e., motives, link together in statement and counterstatement relationships based upon repetition, variation, and contrast.

4. A composite quality of action is created when both voices participate in the rhythmic elaboration. This brings about a smoother and more tightly organized quality of movement.

5. When several cycles of statement and counterstatement of rhythmic motives are carried out, extending over four or more measures, and a point of rest or arrival is reached, the resulting structure becomes a phrase.

EXERCISES

1. Take the following rhythmic motives down from dictation (see pages 55 to 56):

2. Beginning with the following motives, elaborate the upper voice of a cadential formula, using different arrangements of repetition, variation, and contrast (see page 57):

3. Add an upper or lower voice to the following parts, employing motives that will create a composite rhythm (see page 59):

62

4. Using your own motivic material, elaborate cadential formulas in which harmonies have been restated or extended; link several formulas together in some of the exercises (see pages 58 to 59).

5. Reduce the following melodies to their constituent rhythmic motives, and indicate in which ways repetition, variation, and contrast have been used (see pages 56, 58):

Haydn: Sonata in G major (1766), Menuetto, measures 21–28
Beethoven: Symphony No. 2, second movement, measures 1–9
Tchaikovsky: Symphony No. 6, second movement, measures 1–8
Schubert: *Moment Musicale,* Op. 94, no. 3, measures 3–10
Mozart: Sonata in B♭, K. 333, finale, measures 1–8

Chapter Seven

Melodic Elaboration

Rhythmic patterns endow musical sound with momentum and vitality. Melodic patterns guide this momentum through distinctive designs and shapes. These two kinds of elaboration, rhythmic and melodic, combine to give specific profile and character to musical movement.

Three aspects of melodic design will now concern us. These are:

1. The overall shape of the entire melody
2. The melodic motive, the counterpart to the rhythmic motive
3. The relationship of melodic motives and figures to each other

SHAPE OF THE ENTIRE MELODY

No one can be taught to make a beautiful melody. This must be felt deeply within oneself as a meaningful and expressive pattern of the rise and fall of a melodic line. But we can point to certain general features of good melodic design and mention some guideposts which can suggest to the imaginative student ways in which he can set up a firm and coherent melodic framework. This he can then clothe with his own power of invention.

A melody has no required length. It may extend from four through sixteen measures or more. A melodic span incorporates the rise and fall of the melodic line to create interest and yet to maintain unity. The melodic shape is generally highlighted by a point of furthest movement upward or downward. These points are called *apices*. The melodic path to these apices is most often not a straight one; rather the melody rises or falls in one or more curves. In turn, the successive high points of these curves will themselves describe a general movement upward or downward in many cases. Upward and downward movements tend to compensate each other, not necessarily to an equal extent, but sufficiently to provide some kind of mutual balance and to give more detailed profile within the general rise or fall.

In Ex. 1 a number of melodies from musical literature are analyzed according to their general outline, their rise and fall, and their respective apices.

EX. 1. Melodic outlines

a. Beethoven: Symphony No. 5 in C minor, Op. 67, second movement

Andante con moto

long, intense rise to apex at end of melody;

p *dolce*   expected climax   x

b. Mozart: Sonata in A major, K. 331, first movement

double apex followed by two melodic descents; symmetrical but no strong climactic feeling

Andante grazioso

c. Tchaikovsky: Symphony No. 5 in E minor, Op. 64, second movement

Andante cantabile, con alcuna licenza

gradual rise   apex as a sustained climactic plateau
                                          x

dolce con molto espress.

d. Mozart: Sonata in A minor, K. 310, finale

apex (point at which long descent begins)
(marked climax; clearly expected)

Presto   x

e. Schubert: Quintet in C major, Op. 163, finale

apex (end of phrase) somewhat unexpected
                                                  x
Allegretto

p

f. Beethoven: Quartet in C major, Op. 59, no. 3, Menuetto

apex (strong climax; somewhat unexpected)
Grazioso   x

p   3

g. Haydn: Quartet in F major, Op. 77, no. 2, finale

apex (result of counterstatement of first motive step
Vivace assai   higher; no climax yet; occurs later in melody, mea. 7)
                                  x
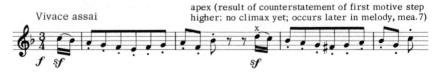

f **sf**   **sf**

As you made rhythmic elaborations upon the basic cadential formulas, especially those formulas which included some extension, you must have been aware of the need to exercise some judgment with respect to the contour of the voices. It may have been necessary, in order to improve the effectiveness of a line of tones, to alter the interval or to extend the harmony. This represents a concern with the melodic aspect of musical composition, specifically, the shape of the melody.

MELODIC MOTIVES; MELODIC FIGURATION

The general outline of a melody is articulated by small melodic figures which are the counterparts of the rhythmic motives we used for the first elaborations. These are *melodic motives,* brief yet distinctive melodic shapes which exercise a very important function in carrying forward musical movement. Melodic motives emerge through the process of *melodic figuration.* Melodic figuration ranges from the most simple type of "fill-in" note to complex and highly substantial clusters of tones which can actually usurp the harmonic function or render the sense of the harmony unclear. Example 2 contains melodies with characteristic types of figuration.

EX. 2.   Melodic figuration in musical literature

a. Beethoven: Quartet in G major, Op. 18, no. 2, first movement

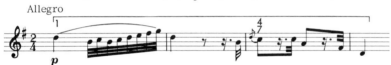

b. Bach: Concerto in E major, first movement

c. Mozart: Sonata in D major, K. 576, finale

d. Chopin: Prelude, Op. 28, no. 21

In general, we find two types of melodic figuration:

1. That which *does not* disturb the underlying harmony
2. That which *does* disturb the underlying harmony

Naturally, the former type of figuration is easier to manipulate and to set into the cadential formula. In this chapter we shall explore the former, i.e., various kinds of tones which are heard after the chord is struck, *while* it sounds; such tones of figuration are generally designated as *unaccented*.

In unaccented figuration the following categories appear:

1. The *neighbor tone*
2. The *passing tone*
3. The *anticipation*
4. The *changing tone*
5. The *escape tone*

In all these categories the tone or tones involved do not belong to the harmony with which they are heard. Another type of figuration elaborates the harmony; this we shall designate as chordal figuration.

1. *The neighbor tone.* This is a tone which lies immediately above or below the harmony tone. The melody line either rises or falls to the neighbor tone and returns to its harmony tone. The neighbor tone is a decorative inflection which gives melodic value to a given level of pitch; it is relatively quiet in its sense of movement. If you should wish to impart a quiet, restrained effect to the melody, neighbor tones would serve your purpose.

EX. 3.   Types of neighbor tones

a. Ornamental

b. Strong melodic stress

c. Incorporated into characteristic motive

d. Ornamental

You will note that some of the neighbor tones in the above examples have been altered. This is possible, often desirable, when the neighbor is a full step away from its harmony tone, especially when a lower neighbor tone is involved. In diatonic major harmony the lower neighbor tones of 2, 3, 5, 6, and 7 may be raised; in minor modes the lower neighbors of 2, 4, 5, and possibly 7 may be raised to good effect. These are illustrated in Ex. 4:

EX. 4.   Raised lower neighbor tones

a. Major: raised 1   *b.* Major: raised 2

c. Major: raised 4   *d.* Major: raised 5

e. Major: raised 6

f. Minor: raised 1   *g.* Minor: raised 3

h. Minor: raised 4   *i.* Minor: raised 6

The raising of a lower neighbor tone adds a nuance of chromatic coloring to the melody; also, it may provide a more intense quality of expression by acting as a kind of leading tone to the harmony note upon which it is dependent. Such special effects must be employed carefully and, as a rule, sparingly. We enjoy the sturdy diatonic quality of the unaltered neighbor tone as much as we may be moved by the "leaning," or "pulling," effect of the altered tone. This general observation applies indeed to all tones of figuration.

For present purposes, the only effective altered upper neighbor is the lowered sixth degree. All other altered upper neighbor tones introduce harmonic problems which we are not yet ready to solve. However, the lowered sixth degree provides a very striking "darkening," which by contrast makes the major harmony sound particularly sweet and gratifying.

EX. 5.   Lowered upper neighbor tones

You will note that the effect of a neighbor tone varies according to its relative length. Some rhythmic motives in the above examples (see Exs. 3*a*, 3*d*) treat the neighbor tone as a slight and elegant decoration. Other examples (Exs. 3*b*, 4*a*, 4*b*) create a considerable amount of rhythmic stress, perhaps involving syncopation. In the latter case, an "expressive" accent is created, and the harmony is somewhat disturbed; the general effect is one of greater musical import.

2. *The passing tone.* The passing tone forms a conjunct melodic connection between harmony tones that lie at different levels of pitch. Passing tones contribute to a smooth quality of melodic movement upward or downward. They are probably the least distinctive of all tones of figuration, creating a rather neutral effect. Unlike neighbor tones, they do not emphasize but often tend to reduce the importance of the harmony tones with which they are linked. In Ex. 6, passing tones in a number of different situations are illustrated. Note that some examples consist merely of "passage" work while others can employ the passing tone to create distinctive motives. The differences lie in the rhythmic patterns and the degree of definition in the melodic shape.

EX. 6.   Passing tones

a. Passage work

b. Motive

c. Expressive emphasis

d. In an extended bass line

Mozart: Sonata in A minor, K. 310, first movement
Allegro maestoso

e. Combined diatonic and chromatic

Mozart: Sonata in C major, K. 330, first movement

Allegro moderato

x = chromatic passing tones filling in a major second
y = diatonic passing tones

3. *Anticipations.* Tones which arrive at the melodic tone of the succeeding harmony before the full change of harmony. Anticipations are generally short in duration and light in accent; ordinarily, they are not longer than the tones from which they proceed. Also, as a rule, anticipations are approached stepwise, but in many cases, they sound highly effective in disjunct melodic patterns. Anticipations can give elegance to a melodic line, and, by binding two principal melodic tones together, they can create a tighter, more driving quality of melodic movement than otherwise would be the case.

EX. 7.   Anticipations

Note the effectiveness of the dotted rhythmic patterns.

4. *Changing tones.* To this point the tones of figuration we have used appear singly between harmony tones, with the exception of a few passing tones. Chord impressions are strong enough to accommodate a more developed kind of melodic ornamentation—a pattern of non-chord tones used in characteristic figures of two or more notes. One such pattern is that of the *changing note.* In a changing-note pattern both the upper and lower neighbor of a chord tone provide the ornament; the melody skips between the two tones, either of which may be sounded first depending upon the context of the melody.

EX. 8.   Changing tones

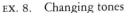

d. Schumann: *Three Piano Sonatas for Young People,* Op. 118, Second Sonata, To Eliza

Changing notes form a decorative pattern. This pattern is anchored at either end or, more commonly, at both ends to the chord tone being decorated. The effect of such tones in a melody is graceful and balanced. Like the neighbor tone, which it resembles, the changing-note pattern tends to reduce the forward drive of melodic action, but it imparts to a given pitch level a more interesting and colorful quality and, of course, extends the pitch level in time.

The order in which the two changing notes occur depends upon the direction of the melodic line immediately preceding and following. No fixed rule can be applied to this procedure. The general curve and flow of the melody and the shape of the melodic figures in the phrase will affect the structure of the changing-note figure. Experiment for yourself, trying different kinds of changing-note figures at a given point in a melody.

5. *Escape tone.* This is a tone which is connected by step to a preceding harmony tone but which leaps to the next harmony tone. The leap is more likely to take a downward direction than upward and is rarely larger than a fifth; often we discover, as in Ex. 9a, that such tones form a pattern of descending thirds. The *reverse* procedure is also available and attractive; that is, a leap to a neighbor tone may be taken after which stepwise melodic motion ensues. In most cases of escape tones and their reverse, a change of melodic direction is recommended. The characteristic feature of these patterns is the melodic gap that precedes or follows the tone of figuration. These tones are especially suitable for imparting an ornamental elegance as well as a distinctive profile to a melodic line. The escape tone and its reverse are illustrated below:

EX. 9.   Escape tones and their reverse

a. Haydn: Sonata in C major, finale

b. Mozart: Andante in F major, K. 533

6. *Chordal figurations.* Much of the melodic action in eighteenth- and nineteenth-century music consists of patterns built on chord tones. Some of the boldest or most elegant melodies in musical literature contain little else

than the tones of a triad; attractive figurations in a prelude, étude, or concerto draw upon chord tones for their melodic material. When combined with sturdy rhythmic action and distributed over a wide range of pitch, chord figures make extremely effective musical sense. Here are some examples from musical literature and also some illustrations of cadential formulas elaborated by chordal figuration:

EX. 10.   Chordal figurations

a. Mozart: Sonata in C minor, K. 457, first movement

b. Bach: Invention in A minor

c. Beethoven: Sonata in C major, Op. 53, finale

d. Schubert: Quartet in A minor, Op. 23, finale

e. Mendelssohn: Symphony in A major, first movement

f.

g.

h.

i.

In analyzing a group of similar motives or figures in a melody we can discover that different kinds of figuration tones are used to construct these similar motives. Thus, anticipations, escape tones, or passing tones, etc., may be used at option provided the general contour and the rhythmic patterns are coherent. Here are some examples:

EX. 11.   Mixtures of tones of figuration

a. Mozart: Sonata in D major, K. 284, third movement

b. Bach: Invention in D major

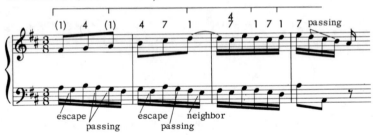

RELATIONSHIP OF MELODIC FIGURES

The melodic material we have been studying exhibits a wide range of style and import. Some of it appears to be highly substantial and distinctive; we hear a well-wrought, impressive theme. Other material has a rather neutral, patterned, filigree effect, consisting principally of passages in quick, even notes. Both these melodic styles are of basic importance in musical composition; often they set each other off in effective contrast; sometimes they may merge or intermingle. In large-scale and complex works, the former type generally serves to indicate areas of departure or arrival in the structure, while the latter serves to give design to music movement. Motives in fully formed themes will tend to show the following relationships:

1. Distinctive rhythmic patterns, involving a variety of note values
2. Variation and contrast in the shape of the figures
3. A A B A, A B A B, A B A C, etc., relationships in the figures

Motives in passage work tend to exhibit the following relationships:

1. Neutral rhythmic patterns, involving many notes of the same brief value
2. Retention of the same melodic shape through a number of motives; or lack of distinctive melodic shape
3. Pairing off of motives as in A A B B C C

EX. 12.   Relationship of melodic figures

Mozart: Sonata in C major, K. 545, first movement

Here are some hints for melodic design:

1. A wide leap is effective, provided it has some counterweight such as a step-wise movement or leap in the opposite direction preceding or following (or both).

EX. 13.   Melodic leaps

a. Haydn: Quartet in F major, Op. 77, no. 2

Menuetto: Presto, ma non troppo

b. Beethoven: Quartet in G major, Op. 18, no. 2, first movement

Allegro

2. Stepwise movement is proper as a general procedure, but it needs a turning effect before the continuous movement in one direction causes the melody to lose its sense of force and shape.

EX. 14.   Stepwise movement

a. Beethoven: Sonata in C major, Op. 2, no. 3, Scherzo

Allegro

b. Mozart: Quartet in B♭ major, K. 589, first movement

Allegro

3. We have seen in many of the examples given above that *repetition* of a melodic tone two, three, or even more times is an effective way of giving a melody a balanced and smooth forward movement.

4. Melodies will gain in coherence and distinction if their constituent rhythmic motives are restated one or more times, by either repetition or variation.

EX. 15.   Repetition of rhythmic motives in a melody

a. Haydn: Quartet in F minor, Op. 20, no. 5, first movement

Allegro moderato

b. Beethoven: Symphony No. 1 in C major, Op. 21, second movement

c. Schubert: Quartet in A minor, Op. 29, finale

In addition to the profile given to a phrase by rhythmic and melodic motives, a characteristic manner can and should be projected. The melodic-rhythmic contour of a phrase is one important value of musical communication; its expressive attitude—one might say, its *affective posture*—is another and probably more fundamental value. Thus, when proceeding to elaborate the basic cadential formulas, you should first try to visualize just what sort of piece you are going to write. Will it be slow, moderate, or quick in pace? Will it have a brightness or darkness of mood? Will it be pitched high or low?

With our present resources the range of affective posture is rather limited. We have available only the more common and familiar dance styles or a rather simple song style. Still, it is possible to project the elegance of a minuet, the briskness of a march, the buoyancy of a gigue or contredanse, the snap of a mazurka, the swing of a waltz, the lyricism of a song. If you can manage to establish a distinctive, convincing impression of one of these familiar types, your elaborations need not be complex or lavish.

The best way to develop a feeling for these types is to perform and listen to examples from music literature and then to make an effort to emulate the manner of each. You will find these types not only in compositions specifically named as dances but in the sonatas, symphonies, quartets, etc., of eighteenth- and nineteenth-century music. Below is a list of dance types to be found in familiar music literature:

Minuet

 Haydn: *London* Symphony, third movement
 Beethoven: Symphony No. 8, third movement

Waltz

 Beethoven: *Archduke* Trio, trio of Scherzo
 Mendelssohn: *Italian* Symphony, third movement

Gavotte

  Haydn: Symphony No. 91 in E♭ major, second movement
  Mozart: Quintet in E♭, second movement

Ländler (German waltz)

  Schubert: Symphony No. 5, trio of third movement

Contredanse

  Schubert: Symphony No. 5, finale
  Beethoven: Quartet No. 1, Op. 18, no. 1, finale

Bourrée

  Mozart: Symphony in G minor, finale
  Bach: *Well-Tempered Clavier,* vol. 1, Fugue No. 2

Gigue

  Beethoven: Concerto for Violin, finale
  Bach: Fugue from Toccata, Adagio, and Fugue in C major

March

  Mozart: Violin Concerto No. 4, first movement
  Haydn: Sonata in C major, first movement

Siciliana

  Beethoven: Symphony No. 6, second movement
  Mozart: Symphony in G minor, second movement

Sarabande

  Bach: *Goldberg* Variations, theme
  Mozart: *Jupiter* Symphony, second movement

Saltarello (quick Italian giguelike dance)

  Berlioz: *Roman Carnival* Overture, allegro section
  Mendelssohn: *Italian* Symphony, finale

Some of these movements actually carry the titles of the dances which they represent. Others use the characteristic rhythmic patterns without a specific designation of any dance type. In both cases, the dance has been the source of the rhythmic style of the piece.

SUMMARY

1. Melodic outline incorporates interesting and unified rise and fall of pitch, highlighted by some kind of apex effect.
2. Melodic motives correspond in length and profile to the distinctive rhythmic motives described in the previous chapter.
3. Unaccented melodic figuration includes the following:

  a. Neighbor tone   *d.* Changing tone
  b. Passing tone   *e.* Escape tone
  c. Anticipation   *f.* Chordal figuration

4. Melodic motives and figures are organized, similarly to rhythmic motives, in statement and counterstatement relationships.

5. Melodic material is generally classified into two types:

a. Distinctive thematic material with well-defined profile and a variety of rhythmic values

b. Neutral "passage" material with less sharp profile and notes of the same rhythmic value, serving to carry forward a harmonic progression and a rhythmic drive

EXERCISES

1. Take the following motives from dictation (upper voice only). Identify the specific kinds of figuration (passing tone, etc.).

Mozart: Sonata in F major, K. 547a, first movement

Beethoven: Sonata in G major, Op. 49, no. 2

Mozart: Sonata in G major, K. 283, first movement

2. Elaborate the cadential formulas given below, first (in *a* through *f*) with various time values and then with the same rapid note values (triplet, sixteenth, etc.), using:

    a. Passing tones (see page 68).
    b. Neighbor tones (see page 66).
    c. Anticipations (see page 69).
    d. Changing tones (see page 70).
    e. Escape tones (see page 71).
    f. Chordal figuration (see page 71).
    g. Similar rhythmic motives using a variety of figuration tones (see page 000).

Cadential formulas for elaboration

Include in the elaborations examples in the styles of minuet, gavotte, bourrée, gigue, contredanse, waltz, sarabande.

    3. Analyze the melodies listed below with respect to the following points:
    a. General contour, apex, secondary contours
    b. Tones of figuration
    c. Relationship of motives
    d. Style of motives

Melodies for analysis

    Brahms: Symphony No. 4, first movement, measures 1–19
    Mozart: Quartet in G major, K. 387, first movement, measures 1–4
    Haydn: Sonata in E minor (1778), finale, measures 1–8
    Beethoven: Quartet in D major, Op. 18, no. 3, finale, measures 1–16
    Schubert: *Moment Musicale* in F minor, Op. 94, no. 3, measures 3–10

Chapter Eight

Three-part Writing;
Fuller Texture

The two parts we have been using in our writing, corresponding to outer voices, have carried the main responsibility for musical action in baroque and classical music. Having dealt exclusively with these voices, we have been able to gain some skill in working out motives, melodic materials, and in shaping units of structure. In doing so, we had shelved temporarily one of the most important values of musical expression, *sonority*. We did this because sonority, notwithstanding its value and importance, had less special value during the baroque and classical eras than had cadential action, rhythmic drive, and melodic contour.

But now that we have set the lines of musical action clearly and will not lose sight of the movement qualities in music, we can begin to clothe the rather bare two-part framework with distinctive and often quite rich qualities of sound. We begin by exploring some of the possibilities of the major triad. Here are some examples of different uses of the C-major triad:

EX. 1.   Sonority effects with C-major triad

g. Beethoven: Sonata in C major, Op. 2, no. 3, first movement

h. Beethoven: Symphony No. 5   *i*. Mozart: Sonata in C major, K. 330,
in C minor, Op. 67, finale   finale

j. Beethoven: Quartet in C major, Op. 59, no. 3, finale

Each of the examples given above has a distinctive sound, indeed, its own expressive impact. As we have said before, often the clue to the general mood of a composition will be given with the first sounds heard.

As we begin to amplify the sound of our music, we add a voice between the soprano and the bass. In so far as sound and chord formation are concerned, this voice can fill out the sound of a triad or repeat a tone of either the soprano or bass.

EX. 2.   Addition of third voice

a. Preferable sonorities   *b*. Acceptable
                                                                                       sonorities

c. Less preferable sonorities

Triads and fuller sounds create a number of problems. How may the tones be placed? Which tones may be doubled? How do fuller sonorities and complete chords relate to the basic harmonic functions we have been study-ing? We begin dealing with these problems by examining triad layouts.

In the following example, three different positions of the C-major triad are given, each with a different tone in the bass part. Then the first two positions are used as the point of arrival for a cadential formula.

EX. 3.   Positions of the C-major triad

a. Root position   *b.* First inversion   *c.* Second inversion

*Six-three is also designated simply as 6.

If you should rate the various positions of the C-major triad according to their effects of stability and instability, you would certainly find $\frac{5}{3}$ to be most stable, $\frac{6}{3}$ less stable but fairly steady, $\frac{6}{4}$ least stable.

Each position of a triad has a certain intrinsic quality of sound that serves coloristic purposes. The firmness and balance of $\frac{5}{3}$; the heightened color and somewhat more opaque quality of $\frac{6}{3}$; the almost cloying, unstable sweetness of $\frac{6}{4}$—each of these has special color value. Here are some examples where composers made particularly effective use of different chord positions.

EX. 4.   Examples of different chord positions

a. Mozart: *Symphonie concertante,* K. 364, first movement

b. Beethoven: Sonata in A major, Op. 2, no. 2, second movement

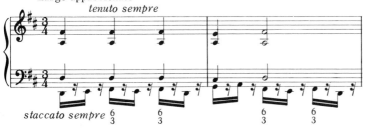

c. Mozart: Quartet in D major, K. 575, first movement

As a rule, $\frac{5}{3}$ acts best for arrival; $\frac{5}{3}$ and $\frac{6}{3}$ chords intermingled accommodate a smoothly moving bass line (quite important within a phrase); $\frac{6}{4}$ chords require special treatment, which we shall describe later. Check the combinations of $\frac{5}{3}$ and $\frac{6}{3}$ chords in the following themes; note where they are used; note especially that the authentic cadence is the one place that $\frac{5}{3}$ dominant and $\frac{5}{3}$ tonic are used with telling effect.

EX. 5.   Five-three and six-three positions in phrases

a. Mozart: Sonata in G major, K. 283, first movement

There is an acoustical reason why $\frac{5}{3}$ sounds stable. The perfect fifth, or its duplicates, the twelfth or the nineteenth, reinforce a natural condition of sound created by the harmonic series (see Chap. 1). This natural perfect fifth is sensed quite strongly when sound is set in motion in the air. Many other intervals are heard from a fundamental, but their effect is much weaker than than of the perfect fifth, with the exception of the octave and major third (heard as a seventeenth). (See Ex. 3*b*, Chap. 4.)

The lowermost note generates the upper notes in the harmonic series. This fundamental tone is called a *root.* By analogy, a triad in which the lowermost tone is placed in the bass is said to be in *root position* (see page 27).

In all our work we shall find the bass to be the strongest and most sensitive tone. It supports the harmony, gives color to the chord, leads the progression forward. If handled skillfully, it adds much style and character to a phrase. If handled ineptly or roughly, it can cause the entire quality of movement to bog down and deteriorate. In your work and in your analysis pay particular attention to the position and action of the bass.

Often the harmonic effect and meaning of a chord is projected sufficiently in three or more parts if only two members of the harmony are present. This depends on the particular circumstances in which the chord is used. For example, suppose we are dealing with a cadential formula within a phrase; two voices are moving in contrary motion to a third voice (Ex. 6).

EX. 6.   Incomplete chords in three-part writing

The first, second, third, fourth, and sixth chords in Ex. 6 are not full triads. In order to accommodate a smooth and attractive melodic pattern, some tones were doubled, leaving no place for the third tone of the triad. Still, the harmonic sense of the progression did not suffer in the least for the absence of full-triad sounds. Briefly, it is possible, even advisable, to use incomplete triads to make good melodic sense at special moments.

In the next example, we have an authentic cadence. The tonic harmony has no fifth. In this case, the root has been *doubled* for two reasons: (1) to make a smooth melodic progression from 7 to 8 in the soprano; (2) to reinforce the sense of finality by emphasizing the sound of the tonic note.

EX. 7.   Root doubled in final chord of authentic cadence

86

Certain tones lend themselves to doubling. Those tones which act for stability are always effective when doubled. These include the roots and fifths of major and minor triads, with root doubling taking preference. Sensitive tones, such as thirds, and either member of the tritone are better not doubled, although the third of a major or minor triad can sometimes be doubled for special effect or to accommodate good voice progression. Here are some examples of doublings:

EX. 8.   Doublings

a. Root

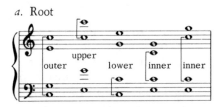 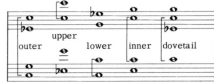

b. Fifth

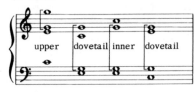 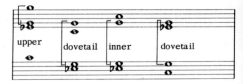

c. Third

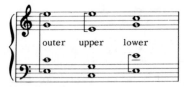 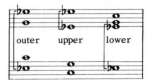

d. Unusual doublings

Beethoven: Sonata, Op. 2, no. 2, second movement

When we distribute the various tones of a chord among the voices, our best guide to spacing is the harmonic series in which larger intervals appear in the lower register and smaller intervals in the upper register. Thus, the best balance in sonority is achieved. Still, when voice leading and smooth chord connection require a different spacing, the balance of the spacing may be altered. In other words, harmonic movement *within* a phrase will take precedence over harmonic sonority; this is not the case at cadences, which require a stable, balanced sound to secure the effect of arrival.

Since we have been dealing with two voices, we have identified intervals by their compass and their function. Now that we are about to use full triads, we employ another system of classification in the intervallic and functional designations. This is the Roman-numeral system of triad classification, which will help us to place a triad within the scale of a key. The system has been described in Chap. 4; it should be used as a guide to the identification of triads but in harmonic importance ranks below the functional aspect, which tells us the exact harmonic meaning of a passage, and the figured-bass aspect, which tells us the degree of weight as well as exactly the composition of a chord. Historically, tonal harmony evolved through functional relationships and figured-bass construction, long before triads were codified by Roman-numeral signs.

ADDING THE THIRD PART

First, we shall add a voice to the two-part exercises we have written. In the following examples, a middle part has been added to two outer parts of cadential formulas given in Ex. 3, Chap. 4. Some are full triads; others omit a tone of the triad; the first triples the root.

EX. 9. Cadential formulas in three voices

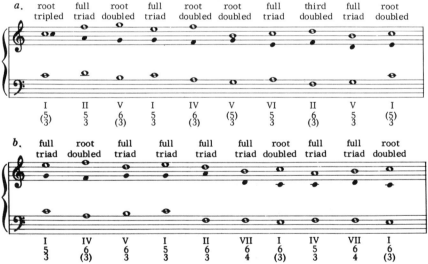

CHORD CONNECTION

As we add voices to the texture, the problem of leading them forward smoothly becomes somewhat more complicated. In Chap. 4 some general remarks regarding the advisability of conjunct movement and common tones were made. Various kinds of movement among the voices were explained; these included parallel, similar, oblique, and contrary movement. When there are three or more voices in a texture, each voice will probably have less range to cover; thus, the recommendation for smoothness of part writing, especially in the middle and lower voices, becomes even stronger. As a rule, it is less effective to lead all voices in one direction than to maintain some oblique or contrary movement. A more interesting and vigorous sense of musical action develops when the movement of voices shows pull in different directions.

While the spacing and texture of chords provides for a wide and varied range of sonority values, still the number of different chords available is rather small. Composers who made use of the chord vocabulary we are learning worked out formulas of voice leading which they applied very consistently throughout their music. There was no hit-or-miss quality about their leading voices. Just as they employed the basic cadential formula and its variants, so did they employ familiar patterns of part writing to connect the harmonies of the formula. In Ex. 10 some illustrations of chord connection are given. These include both simple three-voice progressions and an example from musical literature.

EX. 10.   Chord connection

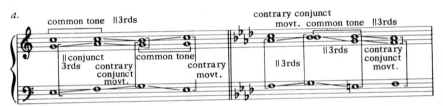

b. Mozart: Fantasia in C minor, K. 475

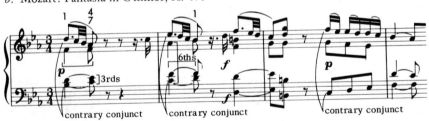

As the texture becomes fuller, conjunct movement in the various voices becomes increasingly important as a means of binding the progression together *and* to change the harmonic meaning with maximum smoothness and efficiency. As we shall see later, in harmony which is concerned with chromatic relationships, stepwise linear action in one or more voices is perhaps the most important factor for musical coherence.

The third voice participates in the processes of rhythmic and melodic elaboration. When we use the third voice, we may elaborate from the three-part chord itself or cause it to pair off with one of the already-elaborated voices of the two-part texture.

In terms of action, the third voice has several possibilities. These are the following:

1. It can proceed as a strengthening or reinforcement of the uppermost voice, exactly or freely.

EX. 11.   Third voice paired with soprano

I   IV   V   I⁶

In this case, it is a *treble* voice, or *alto.*
2. It can proceed as a reinforcement of the bass voice.

EX. 12.   Third voice paired with bass

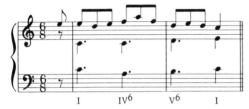

I   IV⁶   V⁶   I

3. It may proceed on its own, either unobtrusively to provide a fuller sound, or with a distinctive life of its own.

EX. 13.   Third voice treated independently

I   IV   V   I

Here and there in a phrase which you may have written, you have felt perhaps that a tone added to the chord or a fourth voice introduced for a measure or two would enhance the effect of your music. Perhaps at the very end you may have wanted both the dominant and tonic harmonies to carry more weight in order to secure the effect of arrival. Provided the doubling does not destroy the balance of the chord, feel free to add where your judgment and taste suggest. One important suggestion concerning the logical handling of free voicing: a new voice may be introduced quite freely, *but* in order to appear logical, it should drop out only after it has reached a point of arrival within the phrase. This point of arrival may be either the conclusion of a cadential formula or the end of a melodic-rhythmic motive. Here are some examples:

90

EX. 14.   Free voicing

a. Beethoven: Sonata in C major, Op. 2, no. 3, second movement

b. Mozart: Sonata in D major, K. 576, first movement

c. Mozart: Sonata in C minor, K. 457, finale

In the fourth and fifth chords of Ex. 14*a,* from Beethoven's Sonata in C major, the bass has been doubled an octave below in order to reinforce the sonority at the half cadence. This does not add a true fifth voice but merely adds weight to the texture. These are not heard as parallel octaves, especially if the doubling takes place to reinforce lower voices.

Free voicing is particularly effective as the music approaches a cadence. The additional weight which a fuller texture creates helps to secure the effect of arrival characteristic of the cadence. Both free voicing and fuller textures are important expressive resources in music. Often we can sense the stylistic and expressive qualities of a composition at first by the impression which the number of voices and their placement give. Both the Sonata in C major, K. 545, of Mozart and the Prelude to *Die Meistersinger* of Wagner begin with the C-major triad. Yet the textures of the two works tell us that they are worlds apart in their expressive qualities. The transparent, middle-level, two-voice texture of the Sonata bespeaks a light and graceful elegance, while the majestic fullness of the Prelude with its relatively low center of textural gravity immediately communicates the noble, serious nature of Wagner's subject.

One final remark about texture is in order here. If you will examine the play of parts in representative choral and instrumental works, you will often find that a voice or part will move above or below the part which is its upper or lower neighbor. This is called *crossing* of voices and is generally brought about by the need of the crossing voice to fulfill a significant melodic pattern of movement. When handled skillfully, crossing of voices can create an interesting and subtle variation of texture and tone color.

EX. 15.   Crossed voices

| I | VII⁶ | I | II VII⁶ I |

The conditions governing doubling as set forth above apply to full three- and four-part chords, where the voices move against each other note by note. When melodic elaboration occurs in the uppermost part (or any other part), doubling is considerably freer. Thus, if the melody outlines the triad, it can touch upon all the tones regardless of whether or not these tones appear in other voices. There is but one condition: as the chord is struck for the first time, the doubling should conform to the conditions set forth above. Example 16 illustrates this point.

EX. 16.   Varied doublings in melodic elaboration

a. Haydn: Quartet in A major, Op. 20, no. 6, first movement

Allegro di molto e scherzando

b. Mozart: Fantasia in D minor, K. 397

Allegretto

c. Mozart: Divertimento in E♭ major, K. 563, second movement

Adagio

SUMMARY

1. Voices added to the basic two-part texture provide the following:
  a. Richer sonority and more complete harmony

b. Reinforcement of upper or lower voice

c. Additional melodic action

2. Five-three positions have the greatest stability; six-three positions have relative stability; six-four positions are decidedly unstable.

3. Doublings depend a great deal upon context; root doubled is strongest effect; fifth doubled is acceptable; third may be doubled provided sonority or voice leading justifies two thirds in a triad; ordinarily, leading tone is not doubled.

4. Occasionally, a chord member may be omitted for smoothness of part writing.

5. Conjunct and common-tone part writing provide the smoothest effect.

6. Different types of part movement between chords maintain a balance and strength of melodic action.

EXERCISES

1. Set the triads B♭ major, E major, D minor, A♭ minor in various combinations of the following specifications (see pages 81 to 86):

a. Three, four, five, six, or eight voices

b. Root position, first inversion, or second inversion

c. Open or closed positions

d. Doubled root, fifth, or third

e. High or low register

f. Voices or keyboard (instruments if available)

2. Add a third (inner) part to cadential formulas composed in connection with the work of Chaps. 4 and 5 (see page 87).

3. Add a third (inner) part to exercises written in connection with the work in Chaps. 6 and 7 (see page 89).

4. Identify, by listening, the position of each of the following triads, and determine which note of the triad is in the uppermost voice (see pages 82, 86):

5. Add fuller texture (two or three more voices) to the following parts (see page 89):

6. Where it seems feasible, add occasional parts in a free-voiced manner to the following phrases (see pages 89 to 91):

Chapter Nine

Rhythmic Patterns of Chord Change

If we were to chart the rhythmic patterns of chord change in most passages, we should find fairly clear and simple patterns involving some kind of balanced or complementary relationship of various time values. These are analogous to the patterns of rhythmic elaboration that we explored in Chap. 6. Below are some examples of chord-change patterns taken from music literature:

EX. 1.   Rhythmic patterns of chord change

a. Haydn: Quartet in A major, Op. 20, no. 6, first movement

b. Mozart: Sonata in D major, K. 576, second movement

c. Beethoven: Sonata in A♭ major, Op. 26, first movement

d. Mozart: Sonata in C major, K. 545, first movement

Allegro

e. Schubert: Quintet in C major, Op. 163, first movement

Allegro ma non troppo

When chords change in complementary patterns, they create larger units of harmonic structure. We hear the entire back-and-forth movement as a harmonic phrase. Such complementary procedures take place on many structural levels, between motives, phrases, periods, and period groups, and contribute significantly to the intelligibility of musical form.

Fluctuation in the relative duration of chords creates its own type of harmonic flow and contributes to the general quality of movement in a musical passage. It may hold back action momentarily, or it may release action; it creates a harmonic ebb and flow within the rhythmic patterns. The variety of patterns used by composers is virtually unlimited. The most we can do here is to indicate some of the possibilities and to establish some general ideas about rhythmic patterns of chord change.

Rhythmic patterns of chord change represent another embodiment of the basic interaction of movement and arrival. Arrival, in the rhythmic sense, is achieved by two means:

1. By greater *length* of a tone in relation to other tones
2. By greater *accent* or emphasis of a tone in relation to other tones

Greater *length* is a relatively mechanical feature of arrival. Any longer note takes on some quality of arrival. *Accent* is normally felt at the end of a phase of rhythmic movement, particularly at the beginning of a measure. These two aspects are illustrated below:

EX. 2.   Rhythmic aspects of arrival

a. Length

b. Accent

c.

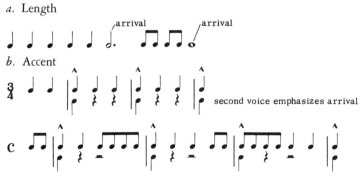

When phases of rhythmic movement are joined, the point of arrival becomes a point of departure. In each sense a rhythmic accent may occur.

Harmonic arrival, as we have come to know, is represented by the tonic harmony which completes a cadential formula. If we combine the rhythmic and the harmonic aspects of arrival in a short passage, giving length, accent to the completing chord of a cadential formula, we achieve a most emphatic and convincing effect of arrival, as in Ex. 3:

EX. 3.   Rhythmic patterns emphasizing cadential arrival

Above, the pattern of chord change acts to bring matters to a close. However, this is not always desirable; in fact, it is only useful at the *end* of a passage. We wish to move forward in music, not to arrive repeatedly with emphasis. Therefore, we arrange the rhythmic patterns of chord change so that rhythmic emphasis and harmonic emphasis do *not* coincide perfectly.

How can this be done?

1. By assigning the chord of arrival to an unstressed point in the measure

EX. 4.   Tonic harmony at unstressed points

2. By passing quickly through tonic harmony

EX. 5.   Tonic harmony of short duration

The concomitant of short tonic harmony, of course, is a longer duration of subdominant or dominant harmony, also illustrated in Ex. 5.

The discrepancy between effects of movement and arrival in rhythm and harmony gives a decided "assist" to musical movement. Control of that movement is achieved by organizing chord changes into rhythmic patterns of *statement* and *counterstatement,* very much like the complementary relationship of motives in rhythmic elaboration of individual chords. Here are some examples:

EX. 6.   Complementary patterns of chord change

a. Beethoven: Violin Concerto in D major, Op. 61, first movement

Allegro, ma non troppo

b. Mozart: Sonata in D major, K. 576, finale

Allegretto

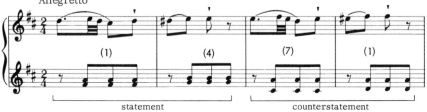

Note in these examples the back-and-forth relationship of tonic and domi-nant harmony, or the pairing off of 1–4 : 7–1. This kind of symmetry creates a larger unit of structure which gathers the two smaller units into a binding statement-counterstatement relationship.

SUMMARY

1. Chords progressing in complementary patterns create larger units of structure.

2. Movement can be maintained by assigning chords of arrival to rhythmically light points and chords of movement to rhythmically strong points.

3. Complementary patterns involving chords of 1, 4, and 7 function prevail in music based on key.

EXERCISES

1. Add figures which are complementary in motive and harmony to each of the figures given below.

a. Add one measure each for (1) and (2), two measures each for (3) and (4). Write two or more solutions for each problem.

b. Complete each exercise so that it becomes a four- or eight-measure phrase ending with an authentic cadence.

(1) Allegro   (2) Andante

(3) Allegro   (4) Adagio

2. Analyze the following excerpts for patterns of chord change and for motive relationship:

Beethoven: Violin Concerto, finale, measures 1–8
Mendelssohn: *Songs without Words,* Op. 85, no. 1, measures 1–4
Schubert: *Rosamunde* Overture, measures 19–26
Mozart: Symphony in G minor, first movement, measures 1–10
Haydn: Symphony No. 102, allegro of first movement, measures 1–8
Brahms: Symphony No. 1, finale, measures 1–8
Mozart: Sonata in C minor, K. 457, finale, measures 1–16
Beethoven: Sonata, Op. 2, no. 1, first movement, measures 1–8

Chapter Ten

The Period

If you should listen for authentic cadences in a movement of a large-scale work by Mozart, Haydn, Beethoven, Brahms, etc., you would find that such cadences are widely spaced and used only at strategic points. Phrases are recognized easily enough, but not all, by any means, end with authentic cadences.

This differs from the procedure we have carried out so far. Most of our phrases arrived by means of authentic cadences. We are now ready to modify our phrase structure in order to create larger forms. In so doing we shall create *periods*.

Listen to the following example:

EX. 1.   Period structure

Mozart: Sonata in A major, K. 331, first movement

We hear two phrases, very similar to each other *except* that the first ends on dominant harmony while the second ends on tonic harmony. This is a *period*, which can be defined very simply as a series of phrases, two or more, which end upon a strong cadence, most often an authentic cadence. The authentic cadence has been likened to the period which ends a sentence; indeed, the entire notion of such a structure as a period is taken over from traditional rhetoric, in which a sentence is described as a period.

Harmonically, larger forms take shape as a series of phrases rounded off by cadences of various kinds. By controlling the effect of arrival so that authentic cadences do not arrest the musical momentum entirely, we can build larger structures than we have so far managed to put together.

Within a sentence, various intermediate points articulate and round off a section of the whole idea being expressed. These may be commas, semicolons, colons, dashes—anything which serves as a point of division or arrival.

Likewise, music has its lesser points of punctuation. Light cadential formulas are less than final in their effect, yet they manage to convey the impression of a segmentation of the flow. Of the lesser cadential points, certainly the most important is the *half cadence;* this involves a pause upon dominant harmony and, of necessity, is involved when the structure incorporates more than one phrase.

We can get some idea of the important role which the half cadence plays in musical structure from Exs. 1 to 4 of this chapter. In these examples the binding action of dominant-to-tonic harmony encompasses an eight-measure structure. The partial effect of arrival at measure 4 creates an effect of suspense which is resolved at measure 8. Indeed, the period form as it is illustrated here becomes a cadential formula which is broadly scaled as follows:

Measure	1	4	8
Chord	I	V	I

Moreover, this cadential formula, based upon the opposition of tonic and dominant harmony, can be much further expanded so as to support very broad forms, such as the sonata form itself, as well as the two-reprise dance and song forms of eighteenth- and nineteenth-century music.

In the half cadence, the dominant chord is best approached by some form of subdominant harmony, although tonic harmony can be used. The following example represents the clearest and least complex relationship of cadences and melodic material in period structure.

EX. 2.   Phrase ending with half cadence

Mozart: Sonata in B♭ major, K. 281, finale

Without doubt, the last chord heard represents a *question* which demands an *answer.* The answer, in this case stated in terms similar to the question, is as follows:

EX. 3.   Phrase answering the one in Ex. 2 with authentic cadence

In its most familiar form, the period consists of two phrases:

1. The first puts a question by means of a half cadence.
2. The second answers the question by means of an authentic cadence.

In the period form we have a larger scale statement-counterstatement relationship than we were able to project in the phrase. The complementary relationship of the two phrases in a simple period is generally carried out in the melodic material. Very often the second phrase is a repetition or variation of the first, modified to make room for the authentic cadence. Other possibilities involve using motives from the first phrase in a different arrangement and, occasionally, contrasting material. Example 1 illustrates the first possibility; in the following examples, we have reworking of the motives and contrast in the second phrases.

EX. 4.   Melodic changes in second phrase

a.

Allegretto

Motives reworked

b. Contrast of motives

Adagio

Returning once more to Ex. 1, you will notice that in the measure before the authentic cadence, the rate of chord change speeds up a bit in order to make room for a full dominant-to-tonic progression. If you listen carefully, you will feel a slight increase in tension because of the quicker harmonic flow. This is a very effective way of preparing for the authentic cadence and enables the composer to round off the period in a satisfying manner. Speeding up the harmony also is effective before the half cadence. The effect, in either case, is that of an increasing drive to the point of arrival.

The impression of balance and symmetry which the two-phrase period creates has been a basic factor in musical structure for centuries. Most dance music—past and present—popular songs, and folk music, as well as much art music, take advantage of this sturdy and useful pattern.

Periods often contain more than two phrases. If the second cadence is not final in effect or if melodic-rhythmic activity continues beyond the point of harmonic arrival, then the period can be extended by one or more phrases. The scale of the extension may sometimes double or triple what would have originally been the length of the period. We shall explore this aspect of musical structure later.

Periods of the type described in this chapter represent perhaps the clearest and most satisfying embodiment of key ever developed in the entire range of Western music. Not only do we have a definite span of time in which we sense the key, but all the events within the period are so organized as to present the key, explore it, and lead us to a final point of arrival which settles us upon the tonic of the key. This, indeed, exemplifies the relationship between harmonic action and large-scale rhythmic structure in eighteenth- and nineteenth-century music. It demonstrates that to create an impression of key takes time; also, that there are various degrees of emphasis in the definition of key. We can summarize these degrees of emphasis as follows:

1. *Indication* of key—the impression given by the opening tonic chord or a single cadential formula. We are told that a given key is very likely to become the theater of the present harmonic action.

2. *Establishment* of key—commitment to the given key through a series of cadential formulas and light cadences throughout the period.

3. *Confirmation* of key—final arrival at the tonic ending the period with relatively strong degree of emphasis.

The interplay of indication, establishment, and confirmation of key involving one or more keys represents the principal element in the harmonic aspects of musical form in eighteenth- and nineteenth-century music. These events take time and provide continuity and coherence par excellence for this music.

SUMMARY

1. The period is formed of a group of phrases which end with a strong cadence, generally an authentic cadence.

2. The typical eighteenth-century period consists of two phrases, the first of which ends with a half cadence, the second with authentic cadence.

3. The material of the second phrase generally is a restatement of the first, but it may involve a contrast as well.

4. Periods create a sense of structural symmetry, and they organize the musical action by directing it to a point of arrival. They also represent the clearest structural embodiments of key in Western music.

EXERCISES

1. Using the musical material from Exercise 3 of Chap. 6 and Exercise 2 of Chap. 7, expand the phrases into periods, with the following layouts:
   a. Two phrases of equal length.
   b. Half cadence at the end of the first phrase, authentic cadence at the end of the period.
   c. Material of second phrase to be either (1) repetition of phrase I or (2) marked contrast.
   d. Two-part texture; subsequently, add a third voice and some free voicing where suitable.

2. Discover various types of period structure in musical literature; ascertain the degree of balance or symmetry, and indicate any departures from normal period structure.

3. Using your own melodic material compose periods in characteristic styles, such as minuet, gavotte, sarabande, indicating what style you have chosen.

Chapter Eleven

The Dominant Seventh;
Six-Four Triad Positions

Musical structures of the eighteenth and nineteenth centuries are to a great extent *periodic* in organization. In order that a phrase, phrase group, period, or larger segment of a composition make proper and complete sense, it must reach its cadence—its "period," or point of punctuation. The stresses built up by various kinds of statements and counterstatements call for some kind of resolution. Such resolutions are provided for by the cadences that act as points of arrival for musical structures in this style.

As structures expand in length, the need grows for cadences of increasing breadth and strength. Thus, a period requires a broader cadence than does a phrase, and a large section or movement calls for entire areas devoted to emphasizing periodic cadential action.

In the eight-measure period, the authentic cadence as we have used it can be quite adequate as a gesture of arrival. In many such periods, however, some broader and more emphatic cadential effect has been introduced. This involves two chord types new to our vocabulary but entirely familiar to us as listeners and performers. These are the dominant seventh and the cadential $\frac{6}{4}$ chords.

In the periods in Ex. 1 observe the chords marked in brackets. In each case, the first of the pair is the cadential $\frac{6}{4}$ chord, while the second is the dominant seventh chord.

EX. 1.   Periods using cadential $\frac{6}{4}$ and dominant seventh at cadences

a. Beethoven: Sonata in G minor, Op. 49, no. 1, finale

b. Mozart: Sonata in C minor, K. 457, finale

In both examples, the combination of the cadential $^6_4$ followed by the dominant seventh gives an impression of breadth and formality to the cadential gesture. This is a very useful and convincing resource when a composer wishes to reach the end of a period or of a much longer section. Examples of this kind of cadence culminating long period groups are found in the following works:

Beethoven: Concerto for Violin, Op. 61, first movement, cadential $^6_4$ measure 75 (period begins measure 51)

Mozart: Quintet in E♭ major, K. 614, first movement, cadential $^6_4$ measures 72–76 (period begins measure 62)

Haydn: Symphony No. 102 in B♭ major, finale, cadential $^6_4$ measures 257–259 (period begins measure 233)

Schubert: Quintet in C major, Op. 163, second movement, cadential $^6_4$ measure 77 (period begins measure 64)

Both the dominant seventh and the $^6_4$ position appear at points other than the formal authentic cadence. In this chapter, we shall examine both these chords and their usage at cadences and within the phrase.

THE DOMINANT SEVENTH

Up to this point we have been using two kinds of dominant action:

1. The *tritone tension,* which creates a drive to tonic harmony
2. The progression of *5 to 1* in the bass voice, which provides a strong effect of arrival in the authentic cadence

When we combine these two aspects of dominant function, we achieve in effect the *dominant seventh* chord, which is spelled as in Ex. 2.

EX. 2.   Dominant seventh chord

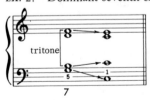

This chord has great power in a cadence to focus harmonic movement to tonic harmony. It is stronger and firmer than the tritone itself; it is more compelling in its cadential drive than the dominant triad, because it takes advantage of the tension created by the tritone.

We cannot mistake the power of this chord to indicate the tonal center to which it owes allegiance. Indeed, the first consistent use of the dominant seventh chord toward the end of the seventeenth century has been regarded by modern theorists as indicative of the crystallization of the present sense of key in music.

The positions of the chord are figured as follows:

EX. 3.   Figured-bass signatures for dominant seventh chord

a. Root position   *b.* First   *c.* Second   *d.* Third
                           inversion   inversion   inversion

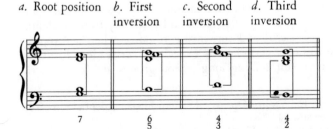

Listen to the two passages in Ex. 4. Note how much more insistently the harmony drives forward in Ex. 4*b* than it does in Ex. 4*a*. There is a bolder projection of key in Ex. 4*b*. The first version uses triads; we hear two chords of the dominant seventh in the second version.

EX. 4.   Settings of a melody

a. Triad setting

b. Setting with dominant sevenths

$$\text{I}^6 \quad \text{II}^6 \quad \text{V}^4_2 \quad \text{I}^6 \quad \text{I}^6 \quad \text{II} \quad \text{V}^7 \quad \text{I}$$

The dominant seventh entered Western harmony by a process of elaboration. It was foreshadowed in one way by a passing tone, as follows:

EX. 5.   Passing tone forming a seventh

$$\text{II}^6 \quad \text{V}^5_3 \, 7 \quad \text{I}^5_3$$

It was more deliberately prefigured by a *suspension* technique, a procedure by which a tone from a chord is held over into the next chord and at that instant becomes a dissonance, as follows:

EX. 6.   Dominant seventh prefigured by suspension

In Chap. 17 we shall examine suspension techniques in detail.

As has been the case with so much melodic elaboration of chords, the tone of elaboration which created a seventh in dominant harmony became incorporated into the chord itself as an integral element. From the earliest medieval times until the twentieth century, the chord vocabulary has grown by the incorporation of tones of ornamentation.

When we write in three-part texture, we must come to terms with the four tones of the dominant seventh. This we do by a process of elimination.

We need the seventh; we need the root. These two make the distinguishing interval of the chord in addition to serving important cadential functions. We also need the leading tone. We do *not* need the fifth of the chord. Although we lose the stabilizing effect of the perfect fifth, we are little concerned with stability at this point; rather, we need the drive and emphasis which the chord provides. Therefore, the root, third, and seventh provide us with a perfectly suitable dominant seventh sound, as in Ex. 7:

EX. 7. Dominant seventh in three voices

$$\text{I} \qquad \text{V}^6 \qquad \text{I} \qquad \text{IV} \qquad \text{II} \quad \text{V}^7 \qquad \text{I}$$

In four or more voices, the fifth is quite important. Not only does it add fullness of resonance to the chord, but it gives it a somewhat richer color, as well.

Chords of the dominant seventh can be used interchangeably with other chords of dominant function. That is, the dominant element in a cadential formula can be represented by the V^7. Since the chord involves leading-tone harmony, the movement of the component members of the chord to the chord of resolution, the tonic, deserves some special attention and consideration.

The fourth degree, as a rule, moves down to 3; the seventh degree, as a rule moves to 8. These are the strong tendencies within the chord. If the chord is used in the authentic cadence, 5 progresses to 1. If a lighter cadential formula is used, the chord may have 7, 4, or 2 in the bass voice. In such cases, 5 is generally held over.

EX. 8. Positions and resolutions of the dominant seventh

$$\text{a.} \qquad\qquad\qquad\qquad\qquad \text{b.}$$
$$\text{IV} \qquad \text{V}^4_2 \qquad \text{I}^6 \qquad\qquad \text{I} \qquad \text{IV}^6 \qquad \text{V}^6_5 \qquad \text{I}$$

c. Mozart: Fantasia in C minor, K. 475

d. Mozart: Sonata in E♭ major, K. 282, Menuetto I

e. Beethoven: Quartet in D major, Op. 18, no. 3, first movement

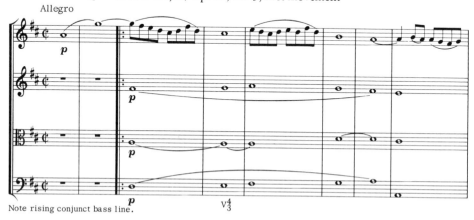

Note rising conjunct bass line.

f. Schubert: Quintet in C major, Op. 163, finale

Note descending conjunct bass line.

110

g. Mozart: Quartet in D major, K. 575, finale

In the inverted positions of the dominant seventh, the resolution to tonic harmony can be very smooth. These progressions involve a minimum of voice movement, but they accomplish a great deal in the way of harmonic action. Indeed, this is a procedure to be recommended highly throughout your entire work in harmony. Try to achieve a strong and effective harmonic shift with subtle and minute shifts of voices from one chord to another. Where a tone can be held over to bind the two chords together, do so if the chord positions will allow. Your progressions will then have an effortless, smooth, but thoroughly convincing flow. Here is an example from Richard Wagner's music, using much more complex harmony than we have yet seen, yet it is bound tightly by the minute and gentle shifts of various parts, as well as by the fact that tones are frequently held over into the next chord.

EX. 9.   Smooth voice leading

Wagner: *Götterdämmerung*

THE CADENTIAL $\frac{6}{4}$

In Ex. 1 of this chapter the chord marked as the cadential $\frac{6}{4}$ serves a very special purpose in the progression. When it sounds, we receive a clear and strong impression that a cadence will be made. This chord is the signal for an authentic cadence and for that reason is designated as the cadential $\frac{6}{4}$.

This chord is built from the tonic triad, with the fifth of the chord in the bass. It has the special quality of being unstable, so that the upper voices, the root and third of the triad, tend to settle downward by step into dominant harmony. Moreover, the especially sweet quality of this position of the triad provides a grateful release of tension following the approach to the dominant in the authentic cadence. Here is the chord and its resolution; it also illustrates the effect of this chord following subdominant harmony.

EX. 10. Cadential $^6_4$

Mozart: Quartet in D major, K. 575, second movement

Subdominant harmony is much the best approach to the cadential $^6_4$. Try the following examples, which use varieties of V, I, and IV. The tightest and most powerful effects come with the use of subdominant harmony.

EX. 11. Approaches to cadential $^6_4$

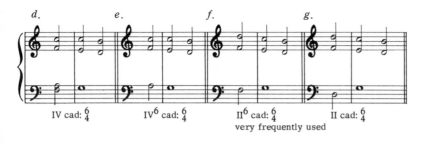

Here are two variants to the basic resolution of the cadential $^6_4$:

1. 8 drops to 7, but 3 rises to 4. This enables the chord to be followed by the dominant seventh and is best used when 8 is in the uppermost voice.

EX. 12.   Variant to the basic resolution of the cadential $\frac{6}{4}$

I⁶   II⁶   cad:$\frac{6}{4}$ V⁷   I

2. Slip the bass down from 5 to 4 as the harmony shifts to the dominant. This lightens the cadence, enabling us to move convincingly past the cadential point of arrival and making possible an extension of the phrase.

EX. 13.   Another variant to the basic resolution of the cadential $\frac{6}{4}$

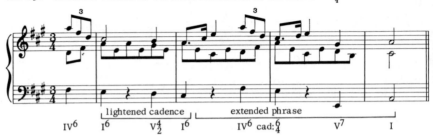

IV⁶   I⁶   V$\frac{4}{2}$ I⁶   IV⁶ cad:$\frac{6}{4}$ V⁷   I

⌞lightened cadence⌟ ⌞ extended phrase ⌟

When four or more voices are used, the fifth of the chord is preferably doubled, then the root. Here are two 4-part resolutions:

EX. 14.   Cadential $\frac{6}{4}$ in four-part harmony

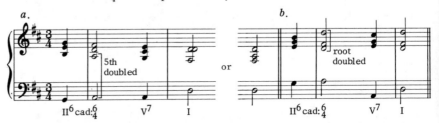

a.   *b.*

5th doubled   root doubled   or

II⁶ cad:$\frac{6}{4}$ V⁷   I   II⁶ cad:$\frac{6}{4}$ V⁷   I

NONCADENTIAL $\frac{6}{4}$ CHORDS

In certain characteristic patterns of harmonic movement, the $\frac{6}{4}$ position of a triad can be used effectively. Each of these patterns involves relatively strong chord positions at both ends; between the strong chords, a neat turn of action can accommodate the unstable sound of the $\frac{6}{4}$ position. These formulas are illustrated below:

1. *Passing* $\frac{6}{4}$. When the bass moves upward or downward by step through

three scale degrees, the middle chord may be a $^6_4$. Here the conjunct movement supports the $^6_4$ sound.

EX. 15.   Passing $^6_4$

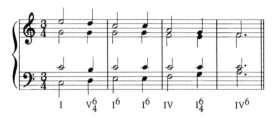

$$\text{I} \qquad \text{V}^6_4 \qquad \text{I}^6 \qquad \text{I}^6 \qquad \text{IV} \qquad \text{I}^6_4 \qquad \text{IV}^6$$

2. *Auxiliary or neighbor* $^6_4$. When a triad is in root position, the two upper voices may effectively pair off to move to their respective upper neighbor tones and then return to the original root-position harmony. The result is a $^6_4$ chord upon the bass tone of the first chord. This effect is frequently used at the beginning of a phrase, especially in eighteenth-century music linked stylistically to the Italian manner.

EX. 16.   Auxiliary $^6_4$

Mozart: Sonata in C major, K. 309, finale

3. *Arpeggio* $^6_4$. If the bass voice has melodic ornamentation of a triadic type, it may create a $^6_4$ position during the course of its action. In such cases, the $^6_4$ position needs to be bracketed by stronger positions of the same chord.

EX. 17.   Arpeggio $\frac{6}{4}$

Schubert: Quintet in C major, Op. 163, finale

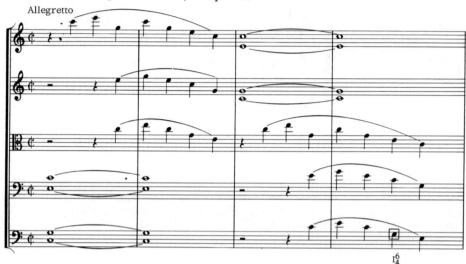

In Ex. 18, the auxiliary $\frac{6}{4}$ of the subdominant triad proceeds to a dominant in the $\frac{6}{5}$ position, instead of returning to the tonic. The smoothness of part writing and the conjunct movement of the bass enable us to use the $IV\frac{6}{4}$ in this manner.

EX. 18. $IV\frac{6}{4}$ in a phrase

SUMMARY

1. The dominant seventh and the cadential $\frac{6}{4}$ create a strong sense of cadence by broader gestures and greater harmonic tension than we have been able to use heretofore.

2. In three voices the fifth of the dominant is omitted.

3. Inversions of the dominant seventh are very useful within the phrase to carry movement forward.

4. The tonic $\frac{6}{4}$ presents a strong signal for a broad cadence when it is sounded near the end of a period or phrase at a rhythmically strong point.

5. Six-four positions may be used within a phrase provided the bass action is either conjunct or stationary or the harmony remains unchanged before and after the six-four.

EXERCISES

1. Identify from dictation the various positions of the dominant seventh which appear in the following passages (see page 106):

Mozart: Sonata in C major, K. 283, second movement

2. Write cadential formulas, in three or more voices, using dominant sevenths in various positions. (See page 108.)

3. Modify the dominant harmony used in previously written phrases so as to create dominant sevenths.

4. Using the following motives, compose periods which incorporate the dominant seventh within the period and at each cadence.

5. Identify, by listening, the various types of $^6_4$ chords included in the following examples (see pages 110 to 114):

Mozart: Sonata in D major, K. 311, second movement

Beethoven: Sonata in F minor, Op. 2, no. 1, Menuetto

Mozart: Sonata in Bb major, K. 281, first movement

6. Realize the following basses in both three- and four-part settings:
(Chord positions other than those figured are to be determined by the student)

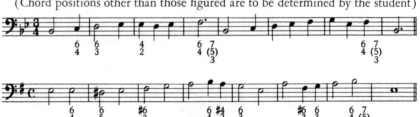

7. Modify the cadences of phrases previously composed so as to include cadential $^6_4$ to dominant seventh action.

8. Using the following four motives, compose periods which incorporate $^6_4$ chord positions of various types.

Chapter Twelve

VII⁷ and V⁹—
The Major Sixth in Dominant Harmony

In the passages in Ex. 1 the chords marked "x" represent dominant-function harmony in which the sixth of the major scale is included.

EX. 1.   Major sixth in dominant-function harmony

a. Beethoven: Sonata, Op. 2, no. 1, second movement

b. Mozart: Quintet in E♭, K. 614, second movement

c. Brahms: Symphony No. 1, Op. 68, second movement

In addition to representing dominant functions, these chords introduce a striking color value into the harmony, sufficiently strong to attract attention as an expressive nuance which can affect the quality of an entire phrase or period.

118

When the dominant note itself is present in the chord, we have the *dominant major ninth,* V⁹.

EX. 2. Dominant major ninth

V⁹

When the dominant note is not present, the chord is designated as VII⁷.

EX. 3. VII⁷

VII⁷

The latter is actually a much more significant chord in the history of harmony than the major ninth chord. Its sound became one of the most important single ingredients in the harmonic language of Wagner and his successors and also pervaded the music of the impressionists, Debussy and Ravel. The famous *Tristan* chord is actually composed of the tones of the VII⁷ as they would appear in F♯ major.

In the harmonic style which we are employing, both the dominant major ninth and the VII⁷ appear rather infrequently. The major sixth degree tends to have a melodic value, as an ornamentation of the fifth degree, rather than a functional purpose. Therefore, when the major sixth degree appears in connection with dominant harmony, it is best used to advantage in the uppermost voice, where its melodic tendency will be realized in a salient manner. Generally, we feel that the progression downward to the fifth degree is the proper or expected resolution of the tone. This takes place before resolution or as the dominant harmony resolves.

EX. 4. Resolution of major sixth in dominant harmony

V⁹   I   V⁹   V⁷   I

In four-part harmony, the fifth of the dominant major ninth is omitted. When the VII⁷ is used, the third of the tonic chord of resolution should be doubled in order to avoid parallel fifths. Various positions of these two chords are available, provided that the major sixth degree is *above* the leading tone and, in the V⁹, that there is the interval of the ninth between the fifth degree and the sixth degree above it. These are illustrated in Ex. 5:

EX. 5.   Positions and resolutions of V⁹ and VII⁷

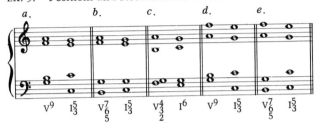

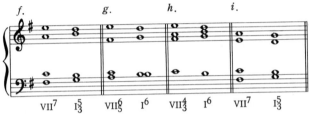

In the next example the sixth degree is treated as the apex of an ornamental chordal figure and proceeds downward by leap to another tone of dominant harmony; this is a very familiar method of incorporating the sixth degree into dominant harmony.

EX. 6.   Sixth degree in dominant harmony used in ornamental chord figure

Mozart: Sonata in D major, K. 576, first movement

The sixth degree in dominant harmony can act as a most convincing melodic apex, focusing all melodic action within a phrase upon a rise toward the high point and a descent from it. In such situations, gradual rise and fall is preferable. In Ex. 7*a*, the harmony moves through cadential formulas to reach the sixth degree; in Ex. 7*b*, the phrase builds up with successively higher levels of dominant harmony.

EX. 7.   Sixth degree as melodic apex

Occasionally, when one voice moves 6–7–8, the harmony momentarily becomes V⁹, with 6 supplanting the leading tone at first. This is illustrated in Ex. 8. The musical effect of this can be quite poised and elegant, as shown below.

EX. 8.   6–7–8 using V⁹

Schubert: Fantasia, Op. 78

Dominant harmony containing the major sixth generally is heard within the phrase. Color, rather than emphasis, is the property of this type of chord. Occasionally, the sixth can be incorporated into final cadential action, particularly if a strong coloristic value is desired.

122

EX. 9.   Sixth degree in final cadential action

Chopin: Prelude in B♭, Op. 28, no. 21

In listening to various forms of dominant harmony we cannot miss the similarities in sonority effect among some of these chords. VII has much of the quality of V⁷, while VII⁷ is akin to V⁹ in effect. For these reasons and for reasons which will be explained below, VII is considered by some theorists to be an incomplete version of V⁷ (i.e., V⁷ minus the root), and VII⁷ becomes an incomplete V⁹.

The reasons for such interpretations probably may be traced to the Rameau system of fundamental bass, in which harmony is considered to be founded on the relationships of triads whose roots lie a fifth distant from the root of the tonic triad. That is, I, IV, and V, *as triads,* constitute the basis of harmony. More complex chords represent additions and elaborations upon the three basic triads, while II, III, VI, and VII represent substitutions for the basic triads. In such a system as the one described it is logical for analysis to refer harmonic phenomena back to the roots of the primary triads.

In the system adopted in this book, based upon intervallic relationships as the fundamental agents of key definition, the issue of determining the Roman-numeral identity of a chord is not the principal point; rather, Roman numerals serve as a convenient and universal means for placing a chord within a key. The function (1–4–7) and the position of the chord (root position, ⁶₃, etc.) tell us more of what we wish to know with respect to the harmonic action and structure than a strict adherence to Roman-numeral root analysis. Accordingly, there seems to be no great need to supply an unheard root to VII and VII⁷.

SUMMARY

1. The major sixth in dominant harmony appears in two chords, the V⁹ and the VII⁷.

2. The sixth degree adds a strong characteristic element of color to dominant harmony.

3. Usually, the sixth degree appears in the uppermost voice, since it possesses marked melodic value.

4. The sixth will tend to resolve downward to the fifth degree, before the dominant harmony moves to tonic *or* at the change of harmony.

5. The sixth may leap downward to another tone of the dominant harmony in a chordal melodic figure, relieving the sixth of the need to be resolved directly.

6. In a 6–7–8 pattern the sixth moves upward to the leading tone, and the V⁹ is first struck without a leading tone.

7. V⁹ and VII⁷ are usually used within a phrase, except in cases described in summary points 5 and 6.

EXERCISES

1. Identify by listening the uses of the sixth degree in dominant harmony in the following passages. Specify chord, position, and resolution of the sixth degree. (See page 118.)

2. Realize the following basses:

3. Using the following motives, compose periods which incorporate the sixth degree in dominant harmony:

Chapter Thirteen

Extending the Period

As listeners, we can take pleasure in appreciating the neat balance of the eight-measure period. When we hear the cadence at the eighth measure, we feel that an orderly and perfectly rounded bit of musical structure has emerged.

Because of this expectation of the cadence it is possible to disrupt the symmetry quite effectively; as a result, the period becomes longer, and musical interest is heightened. Psychologically, the expectation of a cadence is a wonderful opportunity for a composer. He can fulfill that expectation in part, just enough to allow the listener to understand that the music has reached a point of arrival or articulation. But if the arrival is not final, the composer has the opportunity to carry forward with the musical momentum developed in the first part of the period. This is a tug of war between movement and arrival; it can occur dozens, even hundreds, of times within a broad-scale movement, varied and colored in such ways as constantly to hold the listener's interest; yet it allows him to maintain his sense of harmonic direction by indicating the eventual goal, which will be the complete cadence.

In Ex. 1 we give several instances of the disturbance of periodic symmetry at the cadence point:

EX. 1.   Disturbances of phrase balance at cadence points

a. Mozart: Sonata in B♭ major, K. 333, finale

final cadence

b. Mendelssohn: *Songs without Words,* Op. 53, no. 2

The completion effect of the cadence may be lessened in a number of ways. We list some of these methods below and describe them in this chapter.

1. Rhythmic or melodic action can be maintained at the moment at which the dominant harmony resolves to the tonic.

2. A VI chord may replace the tonic chord at the point of resolution. This is the *deceptive* cadence.

3. The authentic cadence may be lightened with respect to the position of the bass; when either dominant or tonic harmony is not in root position, the emphasis of arrival is lessened.

RHYTHMIC OR MELODIC ACTION AT THE CADENCE

In the following examples one or more voices fail to halt their action when the tonic chord is sounded. This suggests that the musical statement has not yet been completed. The material employed in this action may be a melodic figure or the continuation of an accompaniment figure. Sometimes it involves the introduction of new material. In any case, it becomes necessary to repeat at least the cadence, or perhaps to adjoin an entire new phrase in order to create a final effect of arrival.

EX. 2.   Movement carrying past the cadence point

a. Mozart: Quartet in D major, K. 575, finale

cadence point

action in all parts

cadence point

b. Beethoven: Sonata in C minor, Op. 13, finale

final cadence (reinforced)

In both Ex. 2*a* and 2*b* the intention of the composer to extend the period and reinforce the cadence is clear. Many times such action at the cadence of a period is not employed for purposes of extension but to link one period to the material which follows. In these cases, movement forward, not arrival, is the structural procedure. The result in both instances, however, is a broadened dimension in the form, even though sometimes it may not be easy to differentiate between periodic extension and connection between two periods.

DECEPTIVE CADENCE

One of the most effective techniques for delaying the end of a period is the *deceptive cadence*. This involves the substitution of some chord other than the tonic upon the resolution of the dominant in the authentic cadence. Most commonly this chord is the VI, which can represent the tonic function in a cadential formula, as we have learned. Such a resolution does not satisfy our desire to have the complete confirmation of key, and therefore some continuation is mandatory. Eventually, we shall probably arrive at a complete cadence, although in many cases this is not necessarily true. Still, the deceptive cadence makes but one indication, and that is that the music must continue. Later, we shall see how chords other than VI may be used to thwart the resolution.

EX. 3. Deceptive cadence

c. Mozart: Fantasy in D minor, K. 397

(continued)

d. Beethoven: Sonata in G major, Op. 79, second movement

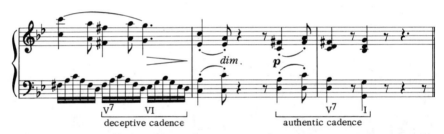

The melodic material which can be used following the deceptive cadence can very easily be a literal or somewhat varied restatement of the two or three measures preceding the deceptive cadence. This would give the impression that the composer is repeating a previous remark in order to correct himself. Example 4 illustrates this:

EX. 4.   Repetition of melodic material after deceptive cadence

Possibly a new motive may be introduced in order to reach the authentic cadence. In this case, a clear and marked contrast is effective, as in Ex. 5:

EX. 5. Contrasted material following a deceptive cadence

Indications for continuation can also be made by lightening the authentic cadence. This is done by substituting some other dominant-to-tonic progression in the bass for the 5 to 1. In Ex. 6, the original phrase would end with a 5 to 1 progression in the bass. The altered cadences proceed, respectively: 4 to 3, 4 to 3, 2 to 1, 7 to 8.

EX. 6. Light cadences and continuations

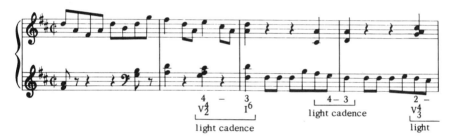

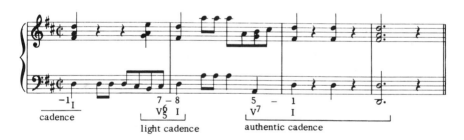

AREA OF ARRIVAL

Part of the compensation that follows upon an inconclusive cadence is the strengthening or emphasis provided by the subsequent authentic cadence. This effect is frequently underlined by restatements of the dominant-to-tonic progression following the authentic cadence itself. By restating the authentic cadence, perhaps with melodic and textural variants, we create an *area* of arrival for the extended phrase.

EX. 7.   Area of arrival at authentic cadence

reinforcements of authentic cadence

THE PLAGAL CADENCE

In much sacred music and in many nineteenth-century works we hear the progression I–IV–I in the area of arrival, often as the very last harmonic progression. This is called the *plagal* cadence. Its effect is that of settling or relaxing harmonic movement in contrast to the driving tension-to-resolution effect of the authentic cadence. Thus the plagal cadence is suitable for the Amen, the "so be it" at the end of a sacred piece, and for the quality of resignation often felt at the end of romantic works, as in Wagner's music dramas, such as *Tristan* and *Götterdämmerung*.

EX. 8.   Plagal cadence

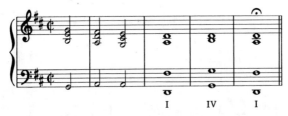

Other chords that represent the subdominant function may be used effectively in the plagal cadence. These will be described in a subsequent chapter.

Example 9 is a complete period into which the techniques for extension have been incorporated and noted. The length of this period has thus been increased from presumably eight measures to twenty-three measures.

EX. 9.   Extended period

Period begins in normal manner with half cadence in mea.4.

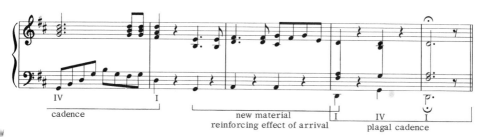

SUMMARY

1. The symmetry of the normal eight-measure period may be broken effectively at the authentic cadence, causing significant extension in the structure of the period.

2. Means of extending periods include:

a. Melodic or rhythmic action at the cadence point.

b. Lighter positions of dominant or tonic harmony.

c. Deceptive cadence.

d. Reinforcement of the authentic cadence by repetitions of the 5 to 1 progression.

e. Plagal cadence.

EXERCISES

1. Determine by listening the type of cadence at the end of each of the following phrases (see pages 127 to 134):

2. Using the motives given below, write four-measure phrases ending with:
a. Authentic cadence.

   b. Light cadence (see page 133).
   c. Deceptive cadence (see page 130).

Motives for phrases

   3. Extend the phrases of Exercise 2 using several nonfinal cadences and concluding with:

   a. Authentic cadence area of arrival (see page 133).
   b. Plagal cadence (see page 134).

   4. Analyze examples of phrase structure in musical literature for the following points:

   a. Length; internal structure of the melody
   b. Cadences; extensions

Chapter Fourteen

The Full Roster of Triads

Our work to this point has been concerned exclusively with the cadential formula, its variants and elaborations. Because of this, we have been able to accomplish the following:

1. We have developed an understanding of the ways in which a key is defined.
2. We have acquired a basic grammar of harmonic progression.
3. We have established structural frameworks for melodic and textural elaboration.
4. We have been able to link harmony to structure within the phrase and period.

There is much diatonic, key-centered, triadic music that does not employ the cadential formula exclusively. Noncadential harmony has attractive expressive qualities quite different from those of cadential harmony. Compare the two following settings of the same melodic line:

EX. 1.   Cadential setting

| I | V | V | | I | VII | I | | V | I | | II | V | I |

But suppose the harmony were lined up as follows:

EX. 2.   Noncadential setting

| I | | III | V | II | | I | VI | VII | III | VII | I | | IV | III | | I | II | | I |

In Ex. 1, we used chords that represented the familiar cadence functions—tonic, subdominant, dominant. In Ex. 2 we used chords that did *not* create a cadential feeling, or for that matter, did not project a strong sense of key; the *scale,* the gamut of C, was clearly indicated, but the tonic C was by no means confirmed. In Ex. 3, we have two passages which use all the triads of the key in turn.

EX. 3.   Use of all the triads in the key

a. Mozart: Sonata in F major, K. 332, finale

b. Mozart: Sonata in D major, K. 576, first movement

We have come to know I, IV, V, V⁷, and VII, also II and VI, as the vehicles of the cadential flow; when these chords were lined up in a certain way, they created cadences and projected the key sense very clearly. In Ex. 2, neither the chords themselves nor their manner of progressing forward accomplished this purpose. Still, these chords belong to the family of triads in a major key and can serve very useful, often striking, purposes within a phrase or period.

Actually, the only triad we have yet avoided has been III; II and VI have served effectively within cadential formulas. III is virtually a stranger to cadential harmony; its diatonic use in later eighteenth-century music is extremely rare, being reserved for certain formulas of chord progression other than cadences. The reason for this, as we indicated in Chap. 4, is that

III makes the leading tone part of an extremely stable interval, the perfect fifth. Thus, it removes from the leading tone the quality of instability or tension which is necessary in the cadence.

In the usual harmonic nomenclature, I, IV, and V have been designated as *primary* triads; this is probably because they give the strongest impressions of key when used together. II, III, and VI have been designated as *secondary* triads. They stand somewhat more remotely from the tonal center and lend a rather obscure color to the key if used frequently or consistently. Here, we shall be concerned principally with one type of procedure, namely, the use of all triads of a major key in patterns, or formulas, of chord progression, as in Ex. 3*a* and *b*.

In each of the following progressions, the chords carry out a line of action, a systematic pattern of movement upward or downward:

EX. 4. Systematic patterns of chord movement

a. Root movement downward by fifth

I   IV   VII   III   VI   II   V   I

b. Root movement downward by third

I   VI   IV   II   III   V   III   I

c. Rising conjunct bass line in first inversion chords

V6   VI6   VII6   I6   II6   III6   IV6   V$^6_5$ I

As you may have noticed, many of the chords used were II, III, and VI; moreover, many chord-to-chord progressions did not fit into our familiar cadential-formula scheme.

Progressions such as the above are very useful within some phrases or periods, especially those involving extension. They operate to good effect in building a drive to a cadence; they also represent effective *continuation* after the first pair of complementary motives has been stated in a phrase or period. This is the plan:

Motive	Linear Pattern	Cadence
Statement and counterstatement	(Described below)	Half or authentic

Example 5 illustrates this plan of structure.

EX. 5.   Phrase using linear pattern

Mozart: Sonata in F major, K. 280, finale

Now, we shall describe some of these linear patterns in detail.

1. *Parallel chords of the sixth*

EX. 6.   Parallel chords of the sixth

Mozart: Sonata in C major, K. 279, finale

Parallel chords of the sixth constitute a technique of very long standing in Western harmony. In English descant and in faux-bourdon of the fourteenth and fifteenth centuries this procedure was used to *widen* and elaborate a given melodic line, and this is still the effect desired when parallel

142

sixth chords are used today, both in instrumental and in vocal music. When the line of sixth chords comes to an end, it is advisable to make some sort of light cadence, although this may be optional according to the sense of the music itself.

2. *Systematic root movement upward or downward by fourth or fifth*

EX. 7.   Bass movement by fourth or fifth upward or downward

a. Bach: *Brandenburg* Concerto No. 5 in D major, first movement

In both examples, the chord roots move in a *circle of fifths*. This kind of bass movement is analogous to that of the authentic cadence. When the bass in root position moves thus, the progression has considerable strength, irrespective of the triads involved. Moreover, as we have seen in the above example, if the direction changes with each progression *and* if fourths and fifths alternate in the bass, a steady and rather massive progression of the harmony upward or downward is achieved. This can provide a remarkably strong element of coherence.

3. *Bass movement in root position upward or downward by third*

EX. 8. Bass movement by third

a. Beethoven: Quartet in G major, Op. 18, no. 2, finale

b.

c. Mozart: Divertimento in E♭ major, K. 563, first movement

Bass movement by thirds is a very smooth, rather subtle kind of progression. Since two tones of the first chord are retained in the second, there is not a marked change in harmonic quality. The effect is one of *sideslipping.* This type of progression is quite effective in leading the music forward without strong cadential or linear action.

EX. 9. Wagner: *Lohengrin,* Prelude to Act I

THE SEQUENCE

In the *sequence,* we find linear action carried out in systematic patterns. A sequence is built of small structural units, ranging in length from one half measure upward, which are restated more or less verbatim on successively higher or lower levels. Every element—rhythm, harmony, melody, texture—participates in the systematic movement upward or downward. The sequence can involve all or most of the triads in a key and can form a substantial part of a phrase or period. Again, like other linear patterns, the sequence functions best as a continuation following a complementary statement of motives. Here are some examples, involving root movement by fourths or by fifths:

EX. 10.   Sequences

a.

I   V   II   VI   III   VII

b. Mozart: Sonata in C major, K. 545, first movement

I^6 IV   VII^6 III   VI^6 II

Note alternation of first inversion and root position chords.

V^6 I   II^6

Examples 6, 8*a,* and 8*c* are also sequences.

Structurally, the sequence can serve a number of purposes. In a baroque concerto, fugue, or sonata, or in a classic phrase or period, the sequence broadens a single phase of movement; its units are no more than a measure or two in length. In a symphony of Mozart or Beethoven, entire phrases or periods are often used as the units for sequential treatment. Each unit is centered upon a different key; the sequence helps, in such cases, to build a large-scale harmonic structure. In the music of Wagner and his contemporaries, the sequence, in addition to carrying musical movement forward, is made to increase the feeling of emotional tension. The sense of drive and accumulation we receive from the sequence is often used by Wagner to build tremendous emotional climaxes, as in the Prelude to his music drama *Tristan und Isolde*.

The full roster of triads covered in this chapter, and particularly II, III, and VI, has been incorporated into systematic linear patterns of chord movement. In nineteenth-century music, noncadential, or nonfunctional, triads have often been used as spots of individual color, possibly as substitutes for the usual cadential chord. While this may introduce an attractive moment in your work, as, for example, if you use III instead of V in a cadential formula, it may seriously weaken the strength of the key impression and, furthermore, may bring in an element of inconsistency unless the effect is matched here and there by similar effects. Here are some examples:

EX. 11.　Noncadential-triad progressions

a. Tchaikovsky: *Nutcracker Suite,* March

b. Liszt: *Années de pèlerinage,* Suisse, Chapelle de Guillaume Tell

c. Mendelssohn: *Hebrides* Overture

SUMMARY

1. Triads within a key may be organized in patterns of noncadential movement as follows:
   a. Parallel chords of the sixth, rising or falling
   b. Systematic root movement by a given interval (fourth, fifth)
   c. Sequences
   d. The substitution of a noncadential chord for a chord of cadential function occasionally or systematically within a phrase or period

2. Well-defined, reiterated patterns of melodic movement or conjunct voice leading in most parts are necessary to make noncadential movement convincing, even more so than with cadential progressions.

3. Patterns of linear movement may replace complementary-phrase structure within a period. These generally will appear after the first pairing of motives and will lead to a periodic cadence.

EXERCISES

1. Identify by listening the type of bass movement in the following progressions. Try to identify the chords by Roman numeral. (See page 140.)

2. Set the following basses with two or three upper voices, adding some elaboration after completing the chordal setting.

3. Complete the progression below in several versions continuing, respectively, with (see page 142):
   a. Sequence by third downward.
   b. Sequence by fourth upward.
   c. Parallel sixth chords downward (see page 141).
Bring the period to an authentic cadence.

4. Set the following melody first with cadential harmony, then with some progressions which are noncadential in style (see page 145).

5. Locate examples of systematic linear patterns of chord movement in music literature.

6. Write several periods in dance style (minuet, gigue, gavotte) using noncadential harmony in (*a*) sequences (*b*) throughout the period.

Chapter Fifteen

Varieties of Texture

Since the time that we began to elaborate cadential formulas rhythmically and melodically we have been concerned with giving our work some distinctive style or manner. We were necessarily limited by the sparse sound of the two-part texture; nevertheless we were able to write exercises in characteristic song and dance styles and to impart something of a positive expressive quality to the music.

Now that combinations of three or more simultaneous sounds are available, the effective range of expression becomes greatly expanded. Fuller sounds can be created; we can work more freely on various levels of pitch; we can broaden the range of total sound to include higher and lower levels; we can set up more complex and interesting relationships between voices. In developing this resource of fuller sound we can explore musical styles that depend for their effectiveness on a richer texture than two voices can provide. In this chapter some of the possibilities of this expanded sonority resource will be explained.

It may well happen that the effort to control a larger number of voices will lead to confusion or to stickiness of part writing. To avoid such difficulties we should remember that we are still dealing with essentially a two-part framework—that in most textures there are generally two important lines of melodic action and that added voices provide a textural elaboration for the purpose of creating a self-sustaining, characteristic sonority. We set our bass and soprano; then we allow the middle voices to take their places in a suitable manner.

Among the varieties of texture we shall describe are the following:

1. Chorale texture
2. Melody and accompaniment
3. Contrapuntal elements

CHORALE TEXTURE

In this texture a compact, rather full sound is the characteristic quality. This comes off best when the performing medium is a group of voices or instruments of similar timbre. A proper blend of sound is important. As a rule, action is slow, and the voices often sound full, sustained chords. Some melodic ornamentation may be introduced, but it is not necessarily continuous; sometimes it may be organized into distinctive motives. Chorale texture generally deals with note-against-note action as the basic relationship between voices. In Ex. 1 a phrase containing a series of cadential formulas is first given; then various types of chorale or choral setting, based upon the harmonic progression of the phrase, are given.

EX. 1.   Chorale settings

a. Chordal setting

b. For instruments: brass, strings

c. Vocal setting, motet style

d. Chorale, baroque style

MELODY AND ACCOMPANIMENT

Melody-and-accompaniment layout is probably the most familiar and useful of all textures. Songs, many short piano pieces, dances, and many passages in concert music consist of a salient melody and an accompaniment which supports and "dresses" it up. A very simple example follows. The phrase in Ex. 2*a* consists of a melody created by elaboration from the uppermost voice of a three-voice texture (the original chord tones are indicated);

the two lower voices remain as they were in the chordal version. In the phrase in Ex. 2*b*, the two lower voices are alternated with each other in a simple eighth-note rhythm. This is called a *broken-chord figure*.

EX. 2.   Chordal versus accompaniment texture

a. Chordal texture

b. Accompaniment texture

The effect of the accompaniment figure is very marked. In contrast to the previous version of the phrase, the change to an accompaniment figure does the following for the music:

1. It lightens the texture.
2. It creates a more flowing quality of movement.
3. It retains, at the same time, the fullness of harmony, the amplitude of sound of the first version.
4. It highlights and dramatizes the melody by setting up a striking contrast between the melody and the lower parts.

Accompaniment figures can become very elaborate, so much so that they can usurp the principal musical role from the upper voice. Sometimes in Wagner's and Brahms's music, the accompaniment element has a genuine melodic life of its own, while in the music of Chopin and Liszt the sonorities projected by brilliant, highly developed figurations quite overshadow at times the rather simple melodies that float on the surface of the sound. Liszt's *Liebestraum* and Chopin's F♯ minor Prelude are thus composed.

The way in which an accompaniment is worked out by the composer depends on the kind of expression he has in mind. To create a proper and smooth accompaniment is no routine task. Indeed, the composer may devote more thought and effort to this problem than to setting up his principal melodic ideas.

In general terms, the composer must decide to what extent an accompaniment will serve either or both of the following purposes:

1. To provide a background, a "curtain" of sound upon which the melody moves

2. To provide rhythmic underpinning or a rhythmic counteraction to the rhythmic action of the melody

In many cases, sonority effects seem to be more important. For example, the accompaniment in Schubert's song *Wohin* provides a steady, light, and murmuring type of background to the simple melody of the voice. On the other hand, the accompaniment in the first variation of the opening movement of Mozart's Sonata in A major, K. 331, provides a rhythmic punctuation to the melodic fragments assigned to the principal voice, the right hand.

These two types are illustrated in Ex. 3:

EX. 3.   Sonority and rhythmic values in accompaniment

a. Sonority effect in accompaniment

Schubert: *Wohin*

b. Rhythmic punctuation

Mozart: Sonata in A major, K. 331, first movement

change to fuller sonority quality

Accompaniment settings for songs will tend to emphasize sonority values, while dance accompaniments must necessarily emphasize the rhythmic aspect.

Most accompaniment figures involve a kind of "spreading out" of a chord. The chord is separated into individual tones at various pitch levels; these tones are sounded in succession according to a rotation decided by the composer. As a chord progresses, its tones move in their given rotation to the proper tones of the next chord.

EX. 4.   Voice leading in accompaniment

Schubert: Impromptu in C minor, Op. 90, no. 1

We have some latitude in working out the pattern of a broken-chord accompaniment. Not every tone or level must necessarily sound in every chord; sometimes the accompaniment may shift for a moment into a genuine melodic figure. Considerable flexibility in part writing arises from the spreading out of the chord in musical space and in time. Still, we should preserve the basic coherence that arises from treating the accompaniment as an "opened-out" chord progression.

Melodically, the figuration of an accompaniment may involve the following:

1. Broken chord, i.e., arpeggio figuration
2. Repeated chord tones, singly or in groups
3. Ornamental tones, such as passing, neighbor, changing tones

In the following example a number of accompaniment figures are illustrated, covering both rhythmic and melodic varieties.

EX. 5.   Types of accompaniment

a. Broken chord (note range of figure)

Mendelssohn: *Songs without Words,* Op. 38, no. 6

b. Repeated-note figure

Mendelssohn: *Songs without Words,* Op. 53, no. 4

c. Ornamental tones (neighbor)

Mozart: Sonata in F major, K. 547*a*, first movement

d. Rhythmic punctuation

Mendelssohn: *Songs without Words,* Op. 53, no. 5

e. Combined broken chord and rhythmic punctuation

Mozart: Sonata in D major, K. 284, Var. VI

The sonority and textural appeal of piano figuration are so strong and direct that certain types of composition are concerned entirely with such figurations. Preludes, études, fantasias, and episodes in piano concertos often consist of intensive play of stereotyped rapid ornamentation. In

154

order to manage such a procedure effectively it would be necessary to cover a wide range of pitch and to deal with harmonies doubled over several octaves. The figuration itself will generally have somewhat sharper profile than the neutral broken-chord figure of an accompaniment. Several examples of this type of figuration follow:

EX. 6.   Prelude types of figuration

a. Chopin: Prelude in F major

b. Chopin: Prelude in D major

c. Chopin: Prelude in F minor

d. Bach: *Well-Tempered Clavier,* Book I, Prelude in G major

e. Bach: *Well-Tempered Clavier,* Book I, Prelude in C minor

CONTRAPUNTAL ELEMENTS

The formal study of counterpoint is a special discipline which is outside the scope of this work. Yet, in every move we make to build up a texture, we are concerned with counterpoint to some extent. Counterpoint involves *counteraction:* melodic lines in different voices describe different patterns, which fit well together; rhythmic action takes place at different instants in different voices, yet combines to create a composite rhythmic effect that satisfies our feeling for movement. The former, i.e., the melodic counteraction, we call *counterline;* the latter, rhythmic counteraction, we call *countertime.* When counterline and countertime are effectively managed in a texture, a distinct and strong quality of counterpoint emerges; this can occur even in a rather simple melody-accompaniment texture. Sometimes this effect can be enhanced by imitation in one voice of a figure heard previously in another.

EX. 7.   Contrapuntal elements in texture

a. Counterline

Mozart: Sonata in D major, K. 576, finale

b. Counterline

Mozart: Sonata in D major, K. 284, Var. V

c. Countertime

Mozart: Sonata in D major, K. 284, Var. VIII

d. Imitation

Mozart: Sonata in C major, K. 545, Rondo

SUMMARY

1. In developing varieties of texture we make greater use of sonority resources, and we explore the interaction of the component voices in a progression. This brings about a greater scope of expressive qualities.

2. In this chapter textures discussed included:

a. *Choral or chorale type for voices or instruments.* This can be elaborated rhythmically or motivically but basically is a note-against-note style.

b. *Melody and accompaniment.* This separates one voice, generally the uppermost, from the remaining voices and assigns to it a leading melodic role, while the other voices coordinate to provide support with background figures.

c. *Contrapuntal elements.* This represents an elaboration of the melody-accompaniment pattern wherein the supporting voices have more distinct melodic profile. This may involve counterline, countertime, imitation, or nonimitation.

EXERCISES

1. Treat the given basses in the following manner:

a. Determine the function and position of each chord.

b. Add two or more voices above.

c. Work out the texture as (1) a choral piece, close position, note against note with some rhythmic action (if you wish, you may fit a text to the music) (see page 149) ; (2) a chorale for instruments (brass, wind, or string) with some melodic ornamentation in each voice (passing tones, neighbor tones) (see page 149) ; (3) a prelude type of piece (see page 154).

2. Add several different accompaniments to the melody below (see pages 150 to 153). Include:

a. Broken-chord figure (see pages 152 to 153).

b. Repeated-note figure (see page 153).

c. Contrapuntal elements (see page 155).

3. Identify by listening the textures illustrated in the following examples:

Chopin: Prelude in E minor
Beethoven: Violin Concerto, finale, measures 1–20
Schubert: Quartet in D minor, second movement, measures 1–8
Mozart: Quintet in E♭, first movement, measures 39–54
Bach: *Brandenburg* Concerto No. 6, first movement, measures 1–17

Chapter Sixteen

Accented Non-chord Tones

The melodic action we created when we elaborated the harmony with interspersed passing and neighbor tones had little if any effect upon the underlying harmonic feeling. When the harmony changed from one chord to another, we were careful to line up all the tones within the chord. Tones of figuration linked chord tones; they appeared *after* the chord was sounded, upon relatively unaccented points. These, therefore, are *unaccented* tones of figuration.

Suppose we shift the passing tone so that it is heard upon the stressed moment, as in the following example:

EX. 1.   Stressed passing tones

a. Unstressed   *b.* Stressed

The effect is markedly different. Each time the chord changes the melodic line is out of harmonic focus. The harmonic picture becomes clear at the unaccented point. Here are some further examples of non-chord tones heard at the point of chord change or at a rhythmic point which is stronger than that of the following note:

EX. 2.   Non-chord tones

Mozart: Sonata in B♭ major, K. 333, first movement

Allegro

The action in these examples creates a sharper and more striking impact than our previous melodic procedures have been able to do. Within a very short space of time the music carries out a tension to resolution, a movement to arrival action. The uncertainty which the non-chord tone creates in the harmony, the instability—these give a gratifying effect to the resolution to the proper harmony of the chord. A microscopic crisis has been met and overcome within the fraction of a second.

All accented non-chord tones share in this harmonic effect. Moreover, this procedure was the wedge which nineteenth- and early twentieth-century harmony drove into the front of traditional harmony; finally, the authority of traditional harmony was destroyed. For, if the stranger, the foreign tone, refused to yield to the chord by moving to one of its tones but asserted itself as equal to the other tones, the emphasis was shifted from cadential function to specific color value. The combination of sounds was important because of its unique quality and not because a definition of key was being made.

EX. 3.   Debussy: Preludes, Book II, Puerta del vino

Permission for reprint granted by Durand et Cie, Paris, France, copyright owners; Elkan-Vogel Co., Inc., Philadelphia, Pa., agents.

However, in traditional harmonic practice, non-chord tones do not assert themselves so boldly. They are dependent, in that they are linked to a chord tone, either which they displace or to which they proceed. Specifically, this means that such tones must be *resolved*. Generally speaking, resolution is a stepwise action of the melodic line, as in the following examples:

EX. 4.   Stepwise resolution of non-chord tones

The non-chord tones in the examples above formed parts of different figures and motives and created different kinds of effect. The variable qualities were:

1. The manner in which the non-chord tone was approached
2. Whether or not the non-chord tone was struck with the chord
3. The relative length of the non-chord tone
4. Diatonic or chromatic quality of the non-chord tone

Of these four variables, the first is the most important; the manner of approach actually classifies the procedure, in the standard harmonic nomenclature. The manner of approach affects the expressive qualities of the music, so much so that it is possible to build a good picture of a musical style by first determining the characteristic way in which non-chord tones are approached.

At present, we shall examine three different ways in which such accented non-chord tones can be approached:

1. *By step (passing tone; neighbor tone)*

EX. 5.   Passing tones and neighbor tones

Mozart: Sonata in A major, K. 331, first movement

2. *By leap (appoggiatura; changing note)*

EX. 6.   Appoggiaturas and changing notes

a. Mozart: Sonata in Bb major, K. 333, finale

b. Beethoven: Sonata in Eb major, Op. 7, second movement

3. *By repetition or anticipation (appoggiatura)*

EX. 7.   Anticipated appoggiatura

Beethoven: Sonata in F minor, Op. 2, no. 1, second movement

Below we shall describe each of these non-chord tones in detail.

ACCENTED PASSING TONES

Of all the tones listed above, the accented passing one has the lightest effect against its harmony. Such tones can be used freely, particularly in the uppermost part. One important consideration in using any accented non-chord tone is the presence of the tone of resolution elsewhere in the chord. A rather sharp clash may be created; sometimes this can be piquant or striking; at other times, it may sound like a misstep in the flow of the music. As a rule, the root or fifth of a major or minor triad will submit well to such treatment; the leading tone and the third of a triad, being especially sensitive tones, are better not treated in this way, unless the line of the melody moves quickly through the chord on a broad sweep upward or downward. Here are some examples:

EX. 8.   Various uses of accented passing tones

a. Equal, short notes

Beethoven: Sonata in E♭ major, Op. 7, finale

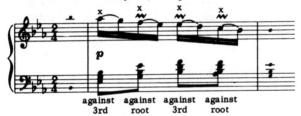

b. Longer than adjacent notes

Mozart: Sonata in D major, K. 576, first movement

c. Chromatic passing tones in pairs

Mozart: Sonata in A major, K. 331, first movement

Observe in the above examples how effective accented passing tones can be in various rhythmic patterns. Equal values, unequal values, long tones, short tones, combinations—all these make good sense within distinctive and well-shaped motives. Chromatic passing tones can enter between two melody tones a major second apart. These provide opportunities for the composer to shape his melody with particular grace and smoothness, as in Ex. 8c.

ACCENTED NEIGHBOR TONES

Accented neighbor tones have the same harmonic obligations as accented passing tones, but the melodic and expressive effect of neighbor tones is quite different from those of passing tones. Since neighbor tones are truly satellites of a single harmony tone, they draw attention to themselves more dramatically than do passing tones, which are links in an ongoing melody. They form characteristic motives which can be used in a series, varied or repeated. They add color to the melodic lines, but they lessen the vigor of the melodic action by establishing momentary levels or plateaus. They invite chromatic inflection even more strongly than do passing tones. Here are some examples of accented neighbor tones:

EX. 9.   Accented neighbor tones

a. Chromatic lower neighbor (longer)

Rossini: *La gazza ladra*

b. Chromatic neighbor tones in pairs (equal)

Schubert: Quartet in D minor, op. post., first movement

c. Ornamental neighbor tones (equal)

Mozart: Sonata in C minor, K. 457

APPOGGIATURAS

Some musical theorists prefer to classify all accented non-chord tones which are struck with the chord as *appoggiaturas*. We prefer here to make distinctions between the above types and the traditional appoggiatura, because of the striking differences in their expressive qualities.

The appoggiatura, translated as a *leaning tone,* is characterized by the fact that it has no preparation. It is approached by leap and often changes melodic direction as it is resolved. Example 10*a* illustrates a prominent, strongly stressed appoggiatura. Example 10*b* contains a number of lightly stressed reverse escape tones (see Chap. 7, Ex. 9) used in a consistent ornamental pattern. These represent appoggiaturas which are virtually a kind of accented unprepared neighbor tone.

EX. 10.   Appoggiaturas

a. Beethoven: Sonata in F minor, Op. 2, no. 2, second movement

b. Mozart: Sonata in D major, K. 284, Var. I

As you can readily hear, appoggiaturas assume great prominence in a melodic line. They impart a strong nuance to the harmony. Their impact is sudden and bold. For these reasons they have a more pointed and intense emotional value than other kinds of non-chord tones. Appoggiaturas make their appearance in great numbers in music of the later eighteenth century and the nineteenth century, where special accents of feeling and sentiment were projected. This was in contrast to the use of non-chord tones in Renaissance and baroque music; music of these two eras preferred non-chord tones in stepwise movement in order to project the melodic feeling of smoothness and consistency, in line with the general feeling of even flow which was desired.

Upward-resolving appoggiaturas invite chromatic inflection. These chromatic nuances color the basic diatonic feeling with an element of poignant sentiment or of slightly restless harmonic feeling, again typical of music of the later eighteenth century.

Each of the melodic ornaments described heretofore has a characteristic effect upon the flow of the music. This effect is qualified by the rhythmic value of the ornament itself. Regardless of the type of ornament, those which are quite short in duration will tend to have a decorative effect, or will act as momentary impediments in the flow of the harmony. Those ornaments which are longer in duration will introduce a stronger nuance, perhaps a more intensely emotional value.

The treatment of melodic ornamentation is a reliable clue to musical style. The unaccented passing and neighbor tones and the deliberate treatment of suspensions characterize Renaissance harmony; bolder treatment of suspensions, seventh chords (see Chap. 17), and a high saturation of melodic dissonances in conjunct movement are found in baroque music; appoggiaturas, often with chromatic inflections, provide a characteristic nuance in classical and romantic music; romantic music tends to place increasing weight and emphasis upon ornamental tones, with respect to both duration and quantity, leading thus to a very rich harmonic color, often mixed and somewhat indefinite in its direction. Twentieth-century music has taken the ornamental figure to be perfectly substantial, treating it often independently of the coexisting harmony or, perhaps, removing the harmonic matrix from which the figure originally grew.

SUMMARY

Accented non-chord tones create a sharp and striking impact upon the harmony. They are classified as follows:

1. Approach by step
a. Passing tones
b. Neighbor tones
2. Approach by leap
a. Appoggiatura
b. Changing note
3. By repetition or anticipation
a. Passing and neighbor
b. Appoggiatura

Accented non-chord tones tend to become increasingly prominent in the music of the nineteenth century, with respect to both number and length. Their importance then overshadows that of their resolutions, until finally the resolution may be omitted entirely and the non-chord tone is accepted into the chord itself.

EXERCISES

1. Identify, by listening, non-chord tones in the following passages:

Mendelssohn: *Songs without Words,* Op. 30, no. 4

Mendelssohn: *Songs without Words,* Op. 30, no. 3

Mozart: Sonata in A major, K. 331, first movement

    2. Elaborate cadential formulas with characteristic motives employing the following tones of elaboration:
    a. Accented passing tones (see page 160)
    b. Appoggiaturas (see page 162)
    c. Neighbor tones (see page 161)
Include both dance and prelude types in your figuration and texture.
    3. Elaborate the material in Exercise 2 into full-scale periods.
    4. Analyze melodies from musical literature, identifying the non-chord tones, their relation to the harmony, and the manner in which they build melodic motives and outlines.

Chapter Seventeen

Suspensions

So far all our non-chord tones have been melodic ornamentations. They have represented an intensified activity in the melodic line.

There is another type of non-chord tone which slows down activity in the melodic line, or in one voice. This comes to pass when one part is held back, when it does not proceed with the others to the next chord. Then, while the other voices are holding to the chord, the belated voice takes its place within the chord, generally moving downward by step. This kind of action is called a *suspension*. Here are some examples:

EX. 1. Suspensions

a. Bach: Chorale, *Christ lag in Todesbanden*

b. Beethoven: Sonata in G major, Op. 14, no. 1, first movement

As you can hear, the effect of a suspension is to bind two chords together by a physical link, not only by a harmonic drive. We hear a miniature crisis, a dissonance, when the suspended part refuses to proceed rhythmically with the others. Then, we have an increased satisfaction when the independent voice clears up the problem by joining the other voices in the chord. Thus, in a suspension, we experience a cycle of stability, instability, stability— in miniature, a departure, a movement, and an arrival phase. Within the span of time allotted to two chords, ordinarily we would have two harmonic impressions if one chord proceeded directly to the next. The suspension, in the same period of time, gives us a three-phase experience, a more intense and compact statement.

For this reason, the suspension has great potentiality for expressive accent. This fact has been recognized for centuries; in Renaissance and baroque music, the suspension was the most important non-chord tone, and its power for intensifying musical expression of various kinds was thoroughly explored. Here are some examples of expressive accent created by the dissonance of the suspension:

EX. 2.   Expressive accents created by suspensions

a. Marenzio: *S'io moro*

b. Bach: B-minor Mass, *Crucifixus*

Suspension action creates emphatic dissonances that possess considerable rhythmic weight. For this reason, a suspension may have as much chordal significance as it has melodic meaning, or more. A historic example of this relationship is the chord of the dominant seventh, in which the seventh of the chord originally often appeared as a suspension from a previous chord. This procedure was evolved in Renaissance and early baroque music. Later, the seventh was incorporated into dominant harmony. Other chords of the seventh and ninth also acquired their "upper" notes by standardization of dissonance combinations originally taken from suspension types. These chords were then classified and used independently.

We find suspensions in many kinds of music, from early Renaissance to late romantic. Expressively, we find a range of style from tightly bound, slow-moving suspensions to highly ornamented suspensions that participate in rapid melodic action. In order to establish the features common to all suspensions, the following outline is given:

1. Stage 1—the *preparation* of the suspension. This involves the presence of the suspended tone in the preceding chord as a member of that chord.

2. Stage 2—the *suspension* itself. This occurs upon a relatively strong metric point as the chord changes.

3. Stage 3—the *resolution* of the suspension. The suspended tone moves by step, generally downward, into its proper place as a member of the chord. Metrically, the resolution is weaker than the suspension itself.

The elements listed above were codified in what has been referred to as the *strict* style, also known as the *stile legato* or the *learned* style. Actually, this style represents a system of counterpoint which was found principally in serious music of the seventeenth and eighteenth centuries, particularly church music. Strict control of dissonance with respect to preparation and resolution is one of the main objectives of the strict style of composition. Opposed to the strict style was the *galant* or *free* style; dissonances were handled with greater freedom respecting preparation and resolution, because of the greater emphasis placed upon ornamental melodic action. We are concerned principally here with varieties of the free style, the basic language of the late eighteenth and early nineteenth centuries in music. Still, whenever suspensions are used in this music, and they appear often, their treatment, perhaps modified, is referable to the conditions governing suspensions in the strict style.

For this reason, our discussion of suspensions will use strict style as a reference. Changes found in the free style will be taken into account, as well.

In order that a suspension make its point, it must provide a sort of stress, or accent, in the musical flow, especially in relation to its resolution. Example 3 illustrates the metrical relationships that allow this emphasis to be realized:

EX. 3.   Metrical relationships in suspension patterns

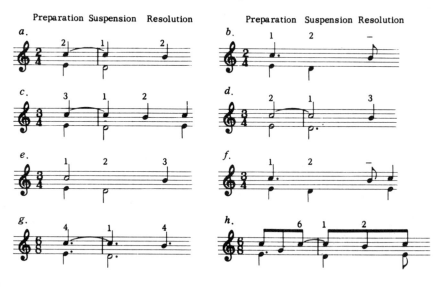

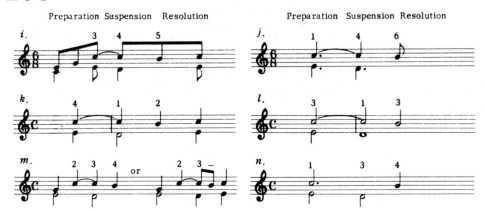

The following chart summarizes the length and accent values:

Phase	Duration	Stress
Preparation	At least as long as suspension	Generally less, possibly equal or greater
Suspension	No longer than preparation	Greater than resolution
Resolution	No longer than suspension	Less than suspension

From the material given above we understand the suspension as an element in the strict style. Music in the free style—dance, soloistic, dramatic—continues to recognize the preparation-suspension-resolution cycle but so modifies the treatment, because of the great range and intensity of motivic action, that the suspension no longer acts as a binder for linear movement; rather, it begins to sound like a melodic ornament such as the appoggiatura. In Exs. 4a through 4d, all drawn from the galant style, melodic and rhythmic modifications of the basic suspension cycle are illustrated:

EX. 4. Modifications of suspension cycle

a. Melodic ornamentation between point of suspension and point of resolution.

Mozart: Sonata in C major, K. 279, second movement

b. The note of the suspension struck with the chord

Mozart: Sonata in D major, K. 284, Var. XI

This provides a strong accent and emphasizes the dissonance, in contrast to the much softer effect of the tied suspension.

c. The preparation much shorter than the suspension

Beethoven: Sonata in F minor, Op. 2, no. 1, second movement

This creates the effect of an anticipated appoggiatura. It can become a very intense expressive nuance in the melody. (See Chap. 16, Ex. 7.)

In this example (Ex. 4*c*) we should be hard put to justify the F in the first full measure as a suspension. Indeed, its preparation is so minimal that we should feel much more correct to describe the tone as an anticipated appoggiatura. Still, this example is important; it has some elements of the suspension cycle and represents the far end of the suspension spectrum, directly opposed to the tied suspension which has a substantial preparation.

d. The preparation itself dissonant to the harmony

Mozart: Sonata in G major, K. 283, first movement

This example is similar to Ex. 4*c* except that the preparation is itself dissonant to the harmony.

Specific suspensions are designated by the interval of dissonance which they create and by the resolution of that dissonance. Further, it is possible to indicate suspensions by signatures in the figured bass which instruct the performer to include certain intervals which create suspensions.

In Ex. 5 we illustrate suspension action in two voices, in order to make the relationship of intervals quite clear. Then, in Ex. 6, suspensions in a chordal texture are given. In these latter examples, the suspension may dissonate against two members of the chord, indicated by two sets of figures.

EX. 5.   Types of suspension

a. 4–3 suspension   *b*. 7–6 suspension   *c*. 2–3 suspension

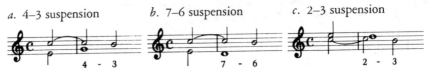

EX. 6.   Suspensions in chordal texture; combinations of suspensions

The 9–8 suspension is rather infrequent in two voices. It is most effective in a full chordal texture, especially when the suspension is in the uppermost voice and the bass takes the tones against which the suspension creates the dissonance. As in other kinds of chordal textures involving suspensions, there will likely be 4–3 or 7–6 suspensions against inner voices.

EX. 7.   9–8 suspensions

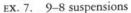

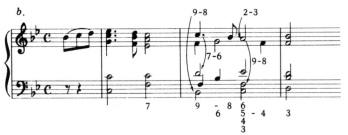

The stepwise contrary motion in 7*a* leads inevitably to the 9–8 suspension.

Suspensions work well in combinations, when two or three notes of a chord are held over while the bass proceeds to the next chord. This is most effective in authentic cadences, broadening the cadential effect and allowing the music to slow down and come to rest smoothly. Note 7–8 here. This is effective particularly in multiple suspensions where 7 is the leading tone.

EX. 8. Multiple suspensions

The time interval between the beginning of the suspension and the point of resolution is usually occupied by the suspended tone itself. However, that time interval can accommodate various kinds of ornamentation, *provided* that we hear the suspension at the proper point and the tone of resolution at its proper point. In other words, we need, as a bare minimum, to touch upon the suspension and its resolution at the proper instants. The remainder of the time interval invites melodic action.

EX. 9. Ornamented suspensions

a. Unornamented   *b.* Anticipated resolution   *c.* Anticipation and neighbor note

d. Repeated suspension tone   *e.* Changing note   *f.* Neighbor tone

g. Neighbor tones   *h.* Arpeggio from preceding chord   *i.* Scale outlining previous chord arpeggio

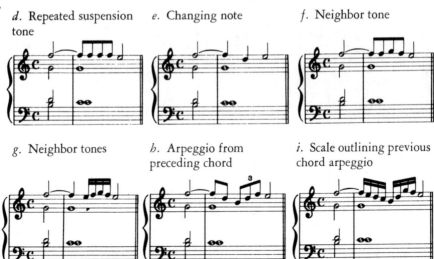

In ornamental suspensions, two kinds of non-chord tone, that which promotes melodic action and that which holds it back, work together.

In suspension patterns some activity can be introduced effectively into the nonsuspended voices. So long as the suspended voice moves properly through its harmonic and melodic steps, other voices can undertake some melodic movement of their own. This can lead to a change of chord upon the resolution of the suspension, as in the following examples:

EX. 10.   Change of chord upon resolution of the suspension

a.

b.

(IV⁶) (VII)   (VI) (IV) (V)   (III) (IV)   (II)

c. Bach: *Well-Tempered Clavier,* Book II, Fugue VI

(II)   (V)

Sequences gain in propulsive power when suspensions are incorporated. Example 11 illustrates these:

EX. 11.   Sequences employing suspensions

a. Suspensions 7–6

b. Suspensions 2–3

Suspensions participate in various kinds of musical action. It is possible to devise opening motives for a period which incorporate one or more suspensions. In such cases, it is likely that the entire period will utilize suspensions motivically in some way, as in the following example:

EX. 12.   Suspensions used in motivic action

Mozart: "Sonata" in F major, K. 533, finale

Cadence points are particularly suited for suspension action, since the slowing down and intensifying effect of the suspension secures the effect of arrival. Both the half cadence and the authentic cadence in Ex. 12 illustrate this effect. Within a period suspensions may be used incidentally to strengthen a progression or to create an expressive nuance. Also, suspensions can be incorporated systematically to good effect in sequences and sequencelike progressions during the *movement* phase of the period's structure.

SUMMARY

1. Suspensions create a slowdown in harmonic movement but increase tension and continuity.

2. There are three phases to the complete suspension cycle:

   a. Preparation; consonant, equal in length to suspension or longer

   b. Suspension; dissonant, at least equal in length and stronger metrically than the resolution

   c. Resolution; consonant

3. The traditional suspensions are 7–6, 4–3, and 9–8 above, occasionally 7–8; 2–3 below

4. Suspensions are effectively ornamented between the point at which they are sounded and the point of resolution.

5. Suspensions may occur several at a time. This is particularly effective at authentic cadence. points when a broad and emphatic impression of arrival is desired.

6. Suspensions enhance the momentum generated in a sequential passage.

EXERCISES

1. Identify from dictation the suspensions included in the following passages:

Mozart: "Sonata" in F major, K. 494, finale

Corelli: *Sonata da chiesa,*
Op. 3, no. 7

Beethoven: Sonata in C minor,
Op. 13, finale

Mozart: Sonata in D major, K. 576, finale

2. Introduce suspensions in the following progressions. Then ornament the suspensions in various ways:

3. Realize the following basses using simple and ornamented suspensions:

4. Using the following motives, compose periods which incorporate various kinds of suspension action. If you wish, proceed with motives you have devised yourself.

Chapter Eighteen

Nondominant Seventh Chords

In the first two beats of measure 1 in Ex. 10*b,* Chap. 17, the combination
E♭, G, D, and later B♭ heard during the suspension sounds like a true
chord rather than a suspension. The tone D, a suspension of the seventh,
can be easily understood as belonging to the chord itself. At this point, we
actually hear a *nondominant seventh* chord.

Suspension action such as we heard in this example can be found very
frequently in music of the seventeenth and eighteenth centuries. At first
such chord forms were understood as types of suspension. Later they were
classified as independent chord forms, among them nondominant seventh
chords. Nondominant seventh chords appear on the first, second, third,
fourth, and sixth degrees of the scale. For our purposes, the most important
common feature of these chords is that they contain no tritone and therefore cannot act as dominant-function chords. In common usage, the most
valuable of these chords is the nondominant seventh on the second degree.
This chord serves a very powerful subdominant function, since it includes
all four tones we have been using in subdominant harmony and creates a
stronger tension pointing to dominant harmony than we have hitherto
been able to muster. Therefore, this chord will be our main concern here.
Conditions regarding its treatment with respect to voice leading apply as
well to other nondominant seventh chords. An example of this chord in
its function as 4 in a cadence is given below:

EX. 1.   Seventh chord on second degree used in cadence

Mozart: Sonata in D major, K. 311, finale

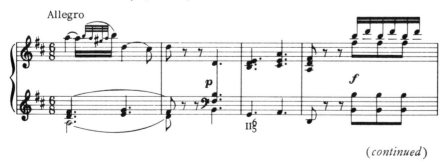

(*continued*)

Like the suspension itself, the seventh of the chord requires preparation and resolution, very much in the same rhythmic and melodic manner as we have observed in the suspension. In Ex. 2 we have four different positions of the chord. Note the especially powerful binding effect of the $\frac{4}{2}$ position as the three upper voices step upward in parallel movement.

EX. 2. Preparation and resolution of nondominant seventh chords

Melodic action in the bass or an upper voice can also create seventh chords. If the bass moves by step downward from the root of a triad while the other voices remain with the chord, a seventh chord is created. Conversely, if an upper voice rises from the fifth of a triad stepwise or by leap, we again have the chord of the seventh. In each of these instances, the seventh will usually be resolved downward by step.

EX. 3. Nondominant seventh chords created by melodic action

b.

$\text{II}^4_2 \qquad \text{VI}^4_2 \qquad \text{II}^7$

Whether a seventh chord be in inversion or root position the most likely resolution is to a triad whose root is a fifth below that of the seventh chord. In this way, the seventh chord and its resolution represent a type of cadential progression, analogous to the progression of the authentic cadence. This applies to all types of nondominant seventh chords.

A very powerful effect of nondominant seventh harmony comes about when the II^6_5 or II^7 precedes the cadential $^6_4$. This broadens the cadential effect; in such a case, we cannot resolve the seventh immediately; it is held over in the $^6_4$ chord and then resolves to the leading tone in the dominant harmony which inevitably must follow. Since the seventh of the II^7 and the fourth of the $^6_4$ are identical, the instability may be carried from one chord to the other, the resolution delayed, and the tension value measurably increased. Several examples follow:

EX. 4. II^7 moving to I^6_4

a. Mendelssohn: *Songs without Words,* Op. 62, no. 4

b. Mozart: Sonata in D major, K. 575, finale

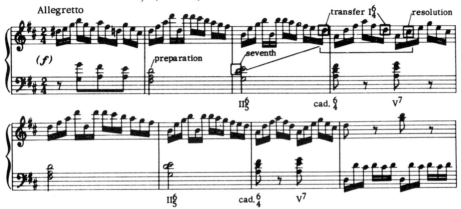

Texture and part writing both affect the manner in which the seventh of the chord is used in the examples given above. In the example from Mendelssohn, we have a seven-part texture; the seventh is tripled for a special brilliant effect of sonority. Only the alto, however, assumes the responsibility for resolving the seventh. In the Mozart example, the voice that first sounds the seventh does not provide the resolution; instead, the principal melodic part, the treble, picks up the seventh in the course of its ornamentation and guides the tone to its resolution. In short, patterns of voice leading, especially those which have strong melodic profile, can bring about satisfactory transfer of resolution of the seventh from one voice to another.

Music of the Baroque and classical eras employs nondominant seventh chords characteristically to support linear patterns and to reinforce cadential action. When the chord roots move in a circle of fifths downward, the most typical pattern, the entire progression becomes a kind of broad cadential formula which circumscribes and defines the key by touching upon every degree; the sense of the key is made especially clear by the presence of the diminished fifth from 4 to 7. Example 5*b* illustrates this procedure.

Linear patterns in seventh chords may also be organized effectively when roots move by thirds, even by seconds (when triads in ⅗ position are also involved). The following examples illustrate root movement by fifth (Exs. 5*a* and 5*c*), by third (Ex. 5*a*); conjunct descending parallel sixths are illustrated (Ex. 5*b*).

EX. 5.   Root movement by fifth, third, and conjunct descending parallel sixths

a. Chains of nondominant seventh chords

b. Dall'Abaco: Trio Sonata, Op. 3, no. 2

Note: this is a borderline situation; ambiguity between suspensions and seventh chords.

c. Bach: Partita in D minor for Violin Alone, Gigue

d. Bach: Invention in G major

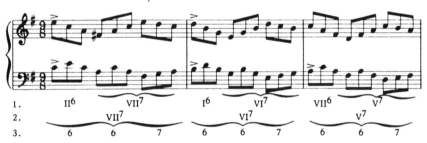

In this final example the figuration involves so smooth a sideslipping by thirds, both downward and upward, that it is possible to accept two different interpretations with respect to chord analysis. These are both given under the example. Line 3 gives the figured bass signatures, which, indeed, were the only concern of Bach himself in harmony, since his music antedates the Roman-numeral system of harmonic analysis.

During the past century the color value of nondominant seventh chords has been used frequently. This is particularly true of impressionistic music and of jazz. In order to make use of such effect we should have to modify the meanings of our harmonic vocabulary quite drastically. The example on the following page illustrates the use of nondominant sevenths coloristically:

EX. 6.   Coloristic use of nondominant seventh chords

Debussy: Preludes, Book I, no. 8, La fille aux cheveux de lin

murmuré et en retenant peu à peu

Permission for reprint granted by Durand et Cie., Paris, France, copyright owners; Elkan-Vogel Co., Inc., Philadelphia, Pa., agents.

Through the sideslipping of parallel $^6_4$ chords and an added upper voice, every form of seventh chord in G♭ major appears in this phrase. The effect is less that of individual chords than of a general impression of movement through the scale of six flats.

SUMMARY

1. Nondominant seventh chords are prepared as follows:
a. As for a suspension; the seventh is held over from a preceding chord.
b. Melodically; the seventh appears as a passing tone or as a tone added to the chord by leap.
2. The expected resolution is downward by step.
3. Nondominant seventh chords reinforce cadential action by adding a tension-resolution element to triadic harmony.
4. The usual progression from a nondominant seventh is to a chord whose root is a fifth below.
5. Nondominant seventh chords operate effectively in sequences, including root movement by thirds and seconds.
6. Nondominant seventh chords have special potential for coloristic use.

EXERCISES

1. Identify, by listening, the manner in which the seventh is approached in the following progressions; ascertain which voice has the seventh. (See page 178.)

2. Add prepared and ornamental sevenths to the nondominant harmony in the following progressions (see page 178):

3. Realize the following basses in four-part harmony. Then, add melodic ornamentation systematically, employing one or two motives repeatedly. (See pages 180 to 181.)

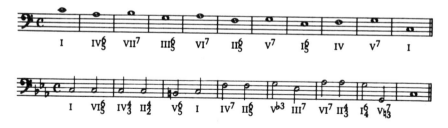

Chapter Nineteen

Special Attributes
of the Minor Mode

Whenever we have composed using the minor mode, we have had to account for the double allegiance of this scale. As a diatonic scale it belongs properly to the major mode beginning on its third degree; as a cadential, key-oriented scale it parallels the major mode beginning on its first degree. We have solved the problem of this ambiguous scale by insisting upon its functional, cadential aspect. We have provided it with a leading tone so that it could represent a key.

The very instability and uncertainty of the minor mode can become a rich source of harmonic action and color. The materials of two key regions can be coordinated and intermingled. For this reason, the minor mode has greater coloristic and perhaps expressive possibilities than the sometimes work-a-day major mode. Shifts, manipulations, contrasts are much more easily and strikingly managed than in the major mode, which gives us but one gamut of seven tones in which to work.

The special attributes of the minor mode include both chords and procedures. They are as follows:

1. Diminished seventh chord
2. Augmented triad
3. Dominant minor ninth chord
4. The natural minor mode
5. The melodic minor mode
6. The Neapolitan sixth chord
7. The tierce de Picardie

ADDITIONAL CADENTIAL RESOURCES

1. *The diminished seventh chord.* In Ex. 1 a type of dominant harmony is used which is new as far as this book is concerned but which is thoroughly familiar to listeners as a harmonic sound. This is the *diminished seventh chord,* a chord built up in thirds from the raised seventh degree of the minor mode.

EX. 1.   Phrase in the minor mode using the diminished seventh chord

Here are some examples of the use of the diminished seventh chord in musical literature:

EX. 2.   Examples of the use of the diminished seventh chord

a. Beethoven: Sonata in C minor, Op. 10, no. 1, first movement

b. Mendelssohn: Symphony No. 3 in A minor, Introduction

As you can hear, the diminished seventh chord has a strikingly characteristic sound: compact, poignant, unstable, and sharply dissonant. It has been used countless times in musical literature to provide an intense expressive accent, as the examples above illustrate. Here is the chord and its resolutions in various positions in the key of D minor:

EX. 3.   Four examples of the diminished seventh chord

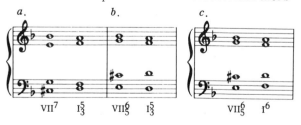

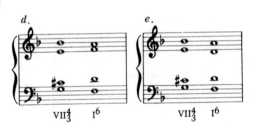

See Ex. 4 for 4–2 resolution.

The diminished seventh chord has a *double* tritone action: between 4 and 7 (the key-indicating tritone) and between 2 and 6, the tritone remaining from the major mode of the key signature. These two, working together, create a very strong pull to the tonic. However, this chord is not entirely satisfactory to represent dominant harmony in the final or authentic cadence. We need the stabilizing power of 5 in the bass to guide us surely home. Therefore, this chord is best used en route, within a phrase or period, to heighten the effect of cadential action, as all our examples above have illustrated.

In Ex. 3, various positions of the diminished seventh chord were given, along with their resolutions. Because of the tritone character of the chord, each note tends to move by step to the tone of resolution. A smoothness of progression is thus achieved, which balances nicely with the sharply dissonant sound of the diminished seventh chord itself. The chord can be used freely in any position but the $\frac{4}{2}$. Here the resolution brings us to a tonic $\frac{6}{4}$, an unstable position, as we know, and one which needs special treatment. Following are two examples of the use of the $\frac{4}{2}$ position of the diminished seventh chord. The first simply takes the bass down a half step to 5 while the upper voices are held over; this gives us a dominant seventh chord. The second takes advantage of a linear pattern in the bass, a descending stepwise line which holds the unstable harmonies firmly in place.

EX. 4.   Resolutions of the diminished seventh in $\frac{4}{2}$ position

2. *The augmented triad*. Note the chord which represents the dominant function in each of the following examples:

EX. 5.   Augmented triads used in cadential formulas

These are *augmented* triads, so described because they are built up with a major third and *augmented* fifth. In the case of the harmonic minor mode, this triad stands on the third degree of the scale. The sound of an augmented triad is unstable, but unlike the diminished seventh, the augmented triad has a gentle, unsettled quality, sweet instead of harsh, diffuse instead of compact. These qualities of the augmented triad arise from the presence of two *major* thirds, F to A, A to C♯, intervals which have a rich and sweet quality of sound. Conversely, the diminished seventh and, for that matter, the diminished triad, both built up entirely by *minor* thirds, partake of the tighter, less sweet quality of the minor third.

We are less likely to find the augmented triad used in a cadential formula, as a substitute for V or VII, than we are to discover it used as a special chord of color, upon any degree, altered where necessary. Here are some examples of the coloristic use of the augmented triad. Note that it makes a very attractive cadence within the major mode.

EX. 6.   Augmented triad used for color purposes

a. Schubert: Fantasia, Op. 15

188

b. Mozart: Sonata in C minor, K. 457, second movement

Eb major   I♮³   IV

Since the augmented triad has two notes in common with the minor tonic, some danger exists of insufficient harmonic action when III moves to I. The leading tone may sound like an appoggiatura, and the listener may not feel a true change of harmony. Thus it may be necessary to lead the voices more actively, and to modify the common-tone formula in such cases. Here are some examples:

EX. 7. Resolutions of the augmented triad

In the final example given above, a very satisfactory alternative is given. III, representing dominant harmony, moves down a fifth to VI, representing tonic harmony. This has something of the strength of the authentic cadence, although the leading tone sounds even more like an appoggiatura than before.

3. *Dominant minor ninth.* In the styles upon which this text is based, the dominant minor ninth is frequently used. The resolutions of the tones of the dominant minor ninth chord are those we have learned in connection with the dominant seventh and the diminished seventh chords. Thus:

EX. 8. Resolution of V⁹ in minor

6 moves to 5.
4 moves to 3.
2 moves to 1 or 3.
7 moves to 8.
5 descends or rises to 1.

This chord is approached exactly as other dominant-function chords, preferably by subdominant harmony, alternatively by tonic harmony. In four voices, the fifth of the chord is omitted. Frequently, the ninth of the chord may be treated as an ornamental tone, dropping to the octave to create a dominant seventh before resolution. Examples of this chord follow:

EX. 9.   Dominant minor ninth

c.

Beethoven: Sonata in C♯ minor, Op. 27, no. 2, first movement

Inverted positions of the dominant minor ninth are feasible, although they are by no means as common as the root position. The characteristic interval of the minor ninth must be retained, regardless of the position of the chord. The sharp dissonance seems to carry more weight when the chord is anchored in root position.

THE NATURAL MINOR MODE

Leading tones are provided in the minor mode in order to give it *structural strength* at cadence points, as well as within the phrase. However, without the leading tone, the minor mode retains its particular minor quality of *color,* and, indeed, when natural 7 is used, some very attractive varieties of effect are available. Here are some examples:

EX. 10.   Minor harmony using natural 7

As you can see, there are three chords which can employ the natural 7. These are III, V, and VII. When these chords are used without leading tone, we no longer have true cadential formulas. Rather, characteristic patterns of voice leading will guide the harmony forward. There are two of particular importance:

1. Descent from 8 through 7 to 6, perhaps beyond
2. Sequences

EX. 11.   Patterns of 8–7–6 movement

The descent through 7 and 6 does not call for a leading tone. In fact, this progression is much smoother and often more convincing in the natural version than in the harmonic or melodic version of the minor mode.

EX. 12.   Sequences in the minor mode

a.

I   IV   VII   III   VI   II   V⁶   I

b. Mozart: Sonata in A minor, K. 310, finale

Presto

In the sequences illustrated above, the entire roster of triads in the minor mode is systematically presented. Thus, the key feeling is thoroughly defined. During the sequences, the natural 7 is used for smoothness and consistency of harmonic color. At the end of each sequence, the period is secured structurally by strong cadence using the leading tone. This is the pattern we can discover in many sequential passages in the minor mode: natural minor within the sequence for evenness of movement; harmonic minor at the end for structural strength.

In Ex. 13, a particularly attractive use of the natural 7 occurs when the melodic line treats the tone as stressed, syncopated apex, so that it becomes the most salient feature of the entire period.

EX. 13.   Mendelssohn: *Songs without Words,* Op. 53, no. 5

THE MELODIC MINOR; THE RAISED SIXTH DEGREE

When the melody rises in a minor key from 5 to 8, through 6 and 7, the leading tone is habitually used to maintain harmonic strength. Often composers wish to avoid the especially strong coloristic nuance which would then arise in the passage from low 6 to raised 7. They then raise 6, creating a diatonic progression identical with that of the major mode. This provides still another variant of nuance in the minor mode; chords used to accommodate the raised 6 can add a special bit of color which contrasts with the low 6 that may have been heard previously in the piece. Here are some examples of the use of raised 6. Note that each of the progressions is a cadential formula of some kind.

EX. 14.   Raised 6 treated chordally

All three versions of the minor scale, natural, harmonic, and melodic, can be used in a purely melodic manner. That is, they can provide melodic elaboration *within* a given harmony. The tendencies of the rising and falling scales make themselves felt in melodic patterns just as they do when the individual tones are harmonized. Here are some examples:

EX. 15.   Melodic variants of the minor scale

a. Beethoven: Sonata in C minor, Op. 13, finale

b. Mozart: Sonata in A minor, K. 310, first movement

c. Mozart: Sonata in A major, K. 331, Alla Turca

CROSS RELATION

In using different versions of the minor scale, we encounter for the first time the harmonic alteration of a tone. Thus, in A minor, we may use both F and F♯, and G and G♯. If the altered and natural versions of the same tone appear in adjacent chords, in different voices, a striking, somewhat edgy, and often unpleasant effect is created. This is called *cross relation,* illustrated below:

EX. 16.   Cross relation

Cross relation can be avoided by assigning both the natural and altered tones to the same voice. In this manner, a very smooth and subtle effect of harmony is created, as below:

EX. 17.   Chromatic progression replacing cross relation

Cross relation is by no means ineffective and has been used by many composers when a strong melodic pattern can accommodate it or when a strikingly bold or edgy effect is in order. (See Exs. 22 and 23.)

We also discover cross relation used quite freely when two melodic lines in the minor mode, one descending from 8 to 5, the other rising from 5 to 8, are heard simultaneously, as in the example below. The clear and strong melodic intention of each part overrides any discrepancy or ambiguity of harmony that may arise from the adjacent or simultaneous sounding of a tone and its alteration; the effect can be quite powerful.

EX. 18.   Natural and melodic minor creating cross relation

THE NEAPOLITAN SIXTH CHORD

In the era before the establishment of the major and minor modes as the standard scales of harmony, a number of scales or modes were used as the basis of tone relationships. These were described above in Chap. 2, page 20. As tonal and cadential feeling developed during the sixteenth and seventeenth centuries, the modes with major third were altered so as to sound like our present major scale. The modes with minor third were altered so as to conform to our present-day concepts of the minor mode. One progression, and indeed, one mode, seemed to have maintained its identity somewhat during this period of change and afterward as well. This was the Phrygian mode, the scale with the sound of a natural minor scale *and* a minor second degree, a half step above the tonic. Cadences in the Phrygian mode were characterized by the half step moving downward, as distinguished from the authentic cadences in all other modes, which were characterized by the upward movement of the leading tone. Here are some examples of Phrygian cadences:

EX. 19.   Phrygian cadences

In Ex. 19c observe that the melodic elaboration creates a cadential formula involving 4, 7, and 1 of E. It is very likely that such elaborations of the Phrygian cadence, expanded and made stronger by harmonic action in other voices, gave rise to what is called the *Neapolitan sixth chord* in standard harmonic vocabularies.

EX. 20.   Elaborated Phrygian cadence giving rise to Neapolitan sixth chord

This chord, in tonal harmony, is a triad, generally standing in the first inversion, involving the lowered second, the fourth, and the sixth degrees

of the minor mode. With few exceptions, it represents the subdominant factor in a cadential formula, as in the following examples:

EX. 21. Various uses of the Neapolitan sixth chord

a. In opening motive

b. Within a phrase

c. As part of the final cadence

Leading the voices in the Neapolitan sixth chord requires special consideration. The tendency of the lowered second degree is to move downward, either by half step or by diminished third, depending upon whether the chord proceeds to a cadential $^6_4$ or to a dominant. Likewise, the tendency of the sixth degree is to move a half step downward. The fourth degree, the least sensitive tone of the chord, may move upward by step, downward by step or third, or remain stationary, depending, of course, upon which chord is chosen to follow the Neapolitan sixth chord.

EX. 22. Resolutions of the Neapolitan sixth chord

a.

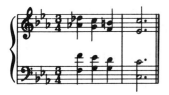

b.   *c.* Cross relation acceptable

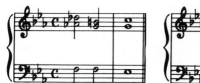

d. Cross relation (D♭–D♮) effective because of sequential motivic pattern

(See also Chap. 23, Ex. 10.)

While the Neapolitan sixth chord needs only three voices, or even two-voice harmony, to be sounded, it is more effective in four parts, in which case the fourth degree is doubled. This four-voiced setup makes it possible to proceed to a cadential $\frac{6}{4}$ chord, as in Ex. 22 above.

Occasionally, the chord on the lowered second degree is effective in root position. Some form of dominant harmony generally follows, as in Ex. 23:

EX. 23.   Neapolitan (sixth) chord in root position

Beethoven: Symphony No. 3, Op. 55, finale

In Ex. 23, the cross relation between the ♭2 and normal 2 is not avoided. In many cases, when they use full harmony, composers add power and tension to the harmony by means of this particular ambiguity. For smoothness of action, the cross relation is best bypassed; for emphatic contrast between subdominant and dominant, the cross relation makes good harmonic sense.

Since the Neapolitan sixth chord has a subdominant function, it may be approached in the manner of a subdominant. It is often preceded by tonic harmony; it may be approached by its own dominant, that is, the sixth-degree triad; we may sound the subdominant chord before it, or, in special situations, use the second-degree triad as the immediate approach to the Neapolitan sixth chord. These are illustrated below:

EX. 24. ·Approaching the Neapolitan sixth chord

a. From I₆

b. From VI

c. From IV

d. From II₆

TIERCE DE PICARDIE

Many compositions written in the minor mode are concluded with the *major* chord of the tonic, instead of the minor. To the listener, this appears immediately as a brightening or sweetening effect. Structurally, this procedure introduces more than a purely coloristic value. As we have already stated, the major harmony and the major mode are the fundamental factors in key-centered harmony. Acoustically, the major triad is more stable than the minor triad. When a composer ends a minor-mode composition in the parallel major, he is strengthening his gesture of arrival; he is putting a firmer seal upon the form and shape of the piece; he is securing the final home position of the tonic. While the major ending does have strong affective value, its greater importance lies in the affirmation of the tonic.

For reasons that have never been clear, such an ending has been given the name *tierce de Picardie*. In nineteenth-century music, especially that of Schubert, we can find instances of the *opposite* procedure, a minor ending to a major work. (See the song *Thränenregen.*) The uncertainty created by this clouding of major harmony is quite in line with the sentimental meaning found in much romantic music. By contrast, it points up the structural role of the major harmony at the end of a minor-mode work.

As a final demonstration of the variety and interest of color that lies within minor-mode harmony, listen to the following period in which all the special effects and values of the minor mode described above are shown.

EX. 25. Period in minor mode

Andante

SUMMARY

1. Special attributes of the minor mode include resources of harmonic function and harmonic color.

   a. The diminished seventh chord: a highly dissonant, unstable version of dominant harmony.

   b. The augmented triad: in the harmonic and melodic minor scales, the augmented triad is found on the third degree; it has a mildly dissonant but sweet quality and can be used to serve a dominant function, but its principal value is as a coloristic nuance.

   c. Dominant minor ninth: a strongly dissonant but firm version of dominant harmony that results from the presence of the fifth (usually in the bass).

   d. The natural minor mode: a version of the minor mode used to accommodate descending melodic motion through 8–7–6; this opens a new area of harmony to the minor mode, adding three triads to the vocabulary and touching upon the *relative* major.

   e. The melodic minor mode: a version of the minor mode used to accommodate ascending melodic motion through 6–7–8; this also adds three new chords to the vocabulary of the minor mode.

f. The Neapolitan sixth chord: the first inversion of a triad whose root is lowered second degree of the minor mode; this chord serves a powerful subdominant function and, because of its altered tone, creates a striking coloristic effect.

g. Tierce de Picardie: the major third in the tonic triad at the end of a piece in the minor mode; this effect represents a stronger confirmation of the tonic than is possible with the minor triad.

2. Below we list the triads associated with each degree of both major and minor modes. The major mode has seven triads available; the minor mode, fifteen:

Triads available in major and minor modes

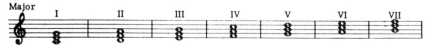

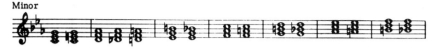

EXERCISES

1. In the following progressions identify, by listening, the various minor-mode procedures or chords which are used:

Mozart: Sonata in F major, K. 332, finale

Chopin: Prelude in C minor

Mendelssohn: *Songs without Words,* Op. 38, no. 2

Allegro non troppo

2. Realize the following basses in three or four parts.

3. Using the following motives, construct phrases:

Chapter Twenty

Expanded Cadential Action

In the following example note the procedures marked with "a" and "x."

EX. 1.   Expanded cadential action

Beethoven: Sonata in A♭, Op. 26, finale

Both procedures represent expansion or intensification of dominant action. At the points marked "a," tones are altered so as to become *leading tones* to chords other than the tonic. The chords of which they are part then become dominants and are described in music theory as *subsidiary, applied,* or *secondary* dominants. The effect of such alterations is to create more intense cadential action than is possible with purely diatonic harmony. Each degree, instead of functioning as a single chord in the key, becomes a temporary focus, a point of arrival with its own cadential formula. It takes on more harmonic weight; in turn, this added weight contributes to a stronger drive forward to the home tonic. The field of action within the key becomes broader; the harmonic is richer and more interesting; in turn, then, the final cadence has a more powerful effect by way of compensating for the preceding digressions.

A secondary dominant can justify harmonic movement between any two triads. This is because tonal harmony accepts the leading-tone tension at face value, independent of texture or voice leading. Thus, we can connect such progressions as I–III, V–II, IV–III, III–II, etc., provided we precede the second chord with its own dominant-function harmony. This condition applies, (see pp. 292-298), to chord progressions involving triads belonging to two different keys. The examples given below illustrate some of these unusual triad relationships justified by applied dominant liaison. Any type of dominant harmony, V, VII, V⁷, VII⁷, V⁹, in a legitimate position may serve in this secondary-dominant role.

EX. 2.   Secondary dominants justifying unusual triad relationships

c. II–III, V–IV

The most useful function of secondary dominants is to reinforce chord progressions which are logical in the scheme of tonal harmony, namely, cadential formulas and systematic patterns of chord movement. In the following example, cadential formulas and sequences are given first diatonically and then with secondary dominants interpolated. Example 4 illustrates secondary dominant use in music literature.

EX. 3.   Cadential formulas and sequences using secondary dominants

EX. 4.   Secondary dominants

a. V of V harmony

Beethoven: Sonata in B♮ major, Op. 22

b. V of IV

Mozart: Sonata in C minor, K. 457, finale

c. Secondary cadential action in a sequence

Beethoven: Sonata in E♭ major, Op. 7, first movement

d. V of II

Mozart: Sonata in B♭ major, K. 281, Rondo

e. V of V

Mozart: Sonata in E♭ major, K. 282, first movement

f. V of V

Mozart: Sonata in D major, K. 311, Rondo

g. Circle of dominants

Schumann: Symphony No. 1 in B♭, Op. 38, first movement

h. V of V to cadential $^6_4$

Mendelssohn: *Songs without Words,* Op. 62, no. 2

(continued)

Secondary dominants not only tighten harmonic action, but tend to broaden basic 1–4–7–1 formulas within the key so that fewer cadences centering on the tonic chord will be employed within a phrase or period. Any point within a phrase or period may be colored or strengthened through the harmonic "leverage" generated by a secondary dominant. In Exs. 1, 4c, and 4g, the sequential action (in one case at the beginning of the period and in the others within the period) is saturated with cadential formulas using secondary dominants. In Ex. 4a, the half cadence is reinforced by the dominant of V. In Ex. 4b, movement to the IV is heralded by V of IV. In Ex. 4d, the period begins "off base" with the V of II. In Ex. 4e, several secondary dominants are used within a period to reinforce cadential movement, while in Ex. 4f, the V of V is used within the first motive to tighten the movement from I to V in a I–V—V–I phrase. In Ex. 4h, the VII⁷ of V serves as a preparation for a broad I⁶₄–V⁷ cadence.

Chord position and voice leading play important roles in the effect created by secondary dominants. In most of the examples given above the chord which represents the dominant function is in a position that promotes smooth movement rather than emphatic cadential punctuation. The bass tends to move stepwise, as do the upper parts; characteristically, common-tone action is present to bind the progression tightly. When a powerful, angular effect is desired or when the composer wishes to place a rhetorical emphasis upon the chord which is to serve as the resolution of the secondary dominant, the 5 to 1 progression in the bass will accomplish the purpose; see Ex. 4g.

Subsidiary leading tones very frequently arise from melodic ornamentation. When the space of a whole tone is filled in melodically with a chromatic passing tone, leading-tone action is created as in many of the examples given above. This is also the case when a neighbor ordinarily a whole step below the chord tone is raised chromatically. In such passing- and neighbor-tone patterns it is a simple matter to define and secure the incipient dominant action by moving one or more other voices to tones belonging to the new dominant. Thus, we see clearly the relation between ornamentation and subsidiary-dominant action. One is elaboration of a tone; the other is amplification of a harmonic position. These are illustrated in Ex. 5:

EX. 5. Passing and neighbor leading tones

PEDAL POINTS

In Ex. 1 at the beginning of this chapter, the sections marked "x" give us dominant harmony over several measures. The effect of the dominant is much more powerful than if it were merely stated and resolved. There is a tension built up which is resolved rather emphatically at the end.

The "x" sections have two distinct features:

1. The retention of the dominant tone in the bass
2. The stepwise movement of the upper voices, *passing* through successive harmonies of the key

The sustained tone is called a *pedal tone,* or *pedal point.* The term pedal refers to the fact that such sustained tones have traditionally been used most effectively in the pedal register of the organ. The upper chords are called *passing chords,* and indeed, they do *pass,* very much as passing tones do. If we were to follow any of the upper voices from the beginning of the pedal passage to the end, we should discover nothing more than a passing-tone figure. One of the important sources of pedal passages was melodic ornamentation over a sustained bass tone. Combinations of neighbor tones or of passing tones tend to group into chords different from the original harmony. Here are some further examples:

EX. 6.   Ornamental harmonies over a pedal tone

a. Mozart: Sonata in B♭ major, K. 333, Rondo

b. Beethoven: Sonata in C minor, Op. 10, no. 1, first movement

c. Mozart: Sonata in F major, K. 332, finale

In eighteenth- and early nineteenth-century usage the dominant and tonic tones were preferred generally for pedal passages. A *dominant* pedal intensifies the drive toward the cadential point, while a *tonic* pedal creates a broad area of arrival. The progression of the harmonies above the pedal tone may be conjunct passing chords, generally of the $\frac{6}{3}$ variety (possibly the $\frac{6}{4}$) as in Ex. 1; they may be grouped into cadential formulas as in Ex. 7 below, which shows first a dominant pedal passage moving in and out of its own dominant and then a tonic pedal over which subsidiary cadential action outlines and amplifies a broad authentic-cadence effect.

EX. 7.   Dominant and tonic pedal points

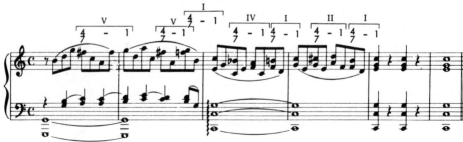

Closely related to pedal action are extensions of dominant harmony. In these the dominant acts as a kind of hub or center around which cadences work. These extensions of dominant harmony may involve any of the following:

1. Alternation of dominant with tonic harmony.
2. Alternation of dominant with its own dominant harmony.
3. Cadential formulas using the dominant as a point of arrival.

These are illustrated below:

EX. 8.   Extensions of dominant harmony

a. Cadential formulas and alternation of dominant with its own dominant

Mozart: Quartet in D major, K. 575, finale

(*continued*)

(I)   (V)   V of home key—I of home key

b. Alternation of dominant with its subdominant (the *home* tonic)

Mozart: Quartet in D major, K. 575, finale

In order to appreciate the scope of dominant and tonic pedal points, we may turn to large-scale music of the later eighteenth and early nineteenth centuries. Listen to the passages listed below, *and* make certain that you hear them in the context of the *entire* movement. Such passages play important structural roles in the form of the entire composition. They focus action *toward* or *upon* important points and areas of *arrival*. As we hear them, we can sense a broadening of gesture proper to important moments in the flow of the music.

Dominant pedal points

Beethoven: Symphony No. 3, first movement, measures 99–109
Beethoven: Symphony No. 3, first movement, measures 603–631 (this includes a digression, in measures 621–627)
Haydn: Symphony No. 103, finale, measures 287–299

Tonic pedal points

Beethoven: *Emperor* Concerto, first movement, measures 564–570
Mozart: Quintet in E♭, K. 614, third movement, measures 50–70

OVERLAPPING SECONDARY DOMINANTS; CONJUNCT BASS LINES

Concentrations of a secondary-dominant action often occur within a period. As each dominant is resolved, a minute cycle of movement and arrival is completed; each point of arrival becomes a point of orientation, and the total effect is one of shifting levels, or plateaus, of harmonic position. If, however, the chord of resolution is omitted or is treated so as to become a dominant-function chord in its own right, a series of *overlapping secondary dominants* is created. The effect of arrival is eliminated; movement is made more intense, and the sense of harmonic orientation is drastically weakened. If anything, such action creates even more powerful drives to clarifying cadential points. Following are some examples:

EX. 9.   Overlapping dominants

a. Mozart: Sonata in F major, K. 332, finale

Allegro assai (♩ = 96)

(continued)

b. Tchaikovsky: *Nutcracker Suite,* Fée dragée

A special application of the subsidiary-dominant procedure involves combining a conjunct, often chromatic, pattern in the bass line with subsidiary cadential action in the upper voices. Here are some examples:

EX. 10. Conjunct bass patterns with subsidiary cadential action

a. Mozart: Sonata in F major, K. 280, first movement

b. Beethoven: Sonata in B♭ major, Op. 22, first movement (sketch of harmonic action)

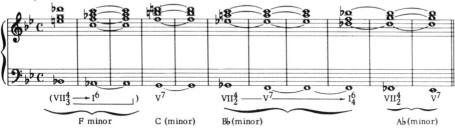

Hundreds of examples of such passages may be found in musical literature, from the sixteenth century to the present day. These progressions are used for different structural purposes. They may be found at the beginnings of periods or farther on, as extensions. Like sequences and parallel chords of the sixth, such passages tend to arrive at half cadences, perhaps themselves extended by pedal points or other means. Here are some examples:

Beethoven: Violin Concerto in D major, Op. 61, finale, measures 297–304
Beethoven: Sonata in D major, Op. 2, no. 2, first movement, measures 58–75
Haydn: Symphony No. 102 in B♭ major, first movement, measures 210–218
Haydn: Symphony No. 103 in E♭ major, first movement, measures 67–73
Mozart: Fantasia in C minor, K. 475, section I
Bach: *Brandenburg* Concerto No. 3, first movement, measures 119–123

The effectiveness of these passages points up once again the importance of linear action, that is, conjunct voice movement, on both the small and the large scales. Conjunct voice movement is particularly critical when chromatic alterations appear. Changes in the position and meaning of a harmony are best supported by smooth and binding melodic action.

As you can hear, pedal points and dominant extensions clearly sound very important. They cannot be easily accommodated in a small, neatly balanced regular period, eight measures in length. Rather, they serve the purpose of pulling the music into line after wanderings, extensions, and instabilities of decided character and scope. Possibly you may be able to incorporate a dominant extension or pedal point into a period already extended by a sequential passage or a deceptive cadence. These are illustrated in the following example, which also includes some subsidiary-cadence action.

EX. 11. Extended period using subsidiary cadential action, dominant pedal points, dominant extensions, and tonic pedal points

Mozart: Sonata in D major, K. 576, finale

Allegretto

FURTHER NOTE ON CROSS RELATION

The techniques studied in this chapter involve alterations of tones. This raises the question of cross relation. As a rule, melodic as well as harmonic considerations call for containing the two tones within the same voice. A melodic rise of two half steps is a powerful binding effect, particularly if the second progression represents leading tone to tonic. This would be lost if the tone and its alteration were assigned to different voices. By the same token, if melodic and rhetorical effects require the use of cross relation to work out a motivic pattern, then the cross relation should appear. Examples of both procedures are given below:

EX. 12.   Cross relation avoided and used

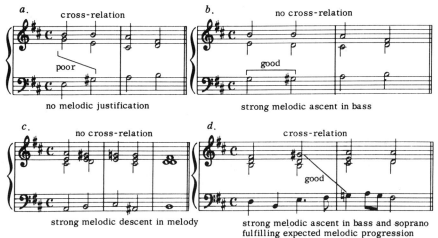

SUMMARY

1. Expanded dominant action includes:

a. Secondary dominants

b. Pedal points on dominant or tonic

c. Extension of either dominant or tonic action by repetition of cadential formulas

2. Secondary dominants tend to reinforce chord progressions within the cadential formula.

3. Secondary dominants may be used effectively to strengthen sequential action or movement through noncadential triads.

4. Stepwise movement in the bass from the secondary dominant to its chord of resolution is recommended in order to facilitate smooth forward action in the harmony.

5. Pedal points broaden cadential formulas. They usually occur at points where key definition can be made on fuller scale, that is, at the beginnings and endings of periods.

6. In phrases of harmonic movement, secondary dominants may overlap, so that each chord of resolution is a new dominant.

EXERCISES

1. Identify, by listening, the secondary dominants appearing in the following passages. Specify the figured-bass position of the dominant and the degree to which it leads.

Mozart: Sonata in F major, K. 332, first movement

Mozart: Sonata in F major, K. 280, second movement

Adagio

Mendelssohn: *Songs without Words,* Op. 102, no. 5

Allegro vivace

Beethoven: Sonata in D major, Op. 28, first movement

Allegro

2. Realize the following basses in four parts:

3. Compose phrases and periods including the following procedures. You may elaborate material previously composed or prepare new material.

   a. V of V (see page 203)
   b. V of IV (see page 203)
   c. V of II (see page 204)
   d. V of VI (see page 203)
   e. Sequence using secondary dominants (see page 203)
   f. Dominant pedal point (see page 207)
   g. Extensions of dominant harmony (see page 209)
   h. Tonic pedal point (see page 208)

4. Analyze examples from music literature using secondary dominants. Specify the type of dominant, the degree to which it resolves, and the role of the progression within the phrase or period.

Chapter Twenty-one

Modulation

Each key in which we have worked has represented a *position* to our musical understanding. A key is a point or area of orientation within the full gamut of musical relationships. Key feeling is projected by a relationship of intervals out of which cadential formulas can be drawn. Thus when we hear a major scale or a phrase based entirely upon that scale, we receive a completely clear impression of a position or of a relationship, and that is what we call the key feeling.

EX. 1.   Sense of key projected by major scale and a phrase

Suppose we change one or another tone in the scale given above:

EX. 2.   Alterations of a major scale; corresponding phrases

In each of these examples we sense a *change* of harmonic position from the original C. A new tonal center is indicated.

This change of position, this shift of tonal center, is the basis of the process called *modulation* in harmony. For us, modulation will open up a broad new world of harmonic color, expanded structure, and intensified cadential action.

First, let us look at some of the general aspects of modulation. Consider the effect upon the form of a period if, instead of beginning and ending in the same key, as we have been doing heretofore, we come to a cadence in another key, as below:

EX. 3.   Change of key at cadence of period

a. Mozart: Sonata in D major, K. 284, Theme and Variations

b. Mozart: Sonata in E♭ major, K. 282

cadence in new key

We have left the home key and have moved out to a new harmonic position; temporarily ʹwe have located ourselves harmonically upon this new point. By *starting out* in one key and *finishing* in another we have established a *contrast* of tonal centers. Harmonically, this is much more interesting and challenging than remaining at home in the tonic.

But this deliberate shift of tonal center creates some questions. It does not satisfy our demand for completion and full stability. It is as if a question were asked, an answer demanded, a statement presented that required counterstatement. The impression of the first key remains with us, in the background, and somehow that impression must be reckoned with; somehow the contrast of the two keys must be reconciled.

In order to provide the answer to the harmonic question created by the modulation, we must proceed further. A compensating period must follow, a period which goes forward from the point of removal, back to the home key, and which settles the issue with a firm authentic cadential statement in the tonic, the original harmonic position. This takes place in the example given below:

EX. 4.   Departure and return involving shifts of tonal center

Mozart: Sonata in D major, K. 284, Theme and Variations

shift to new key

(*continued*)

By such contrast of tonal centers, we have created a harmonic momentum that carries far beyond the point where the contrast was actually made. The musical thought is extended, the structure is built out, and the whole piece takes on a different contour than if it had remained in the home key throughout. The following diagram illustrates this point graphically:

EX. 5. Diagram of the contours of nonmodulating and modulating harmonic schemes

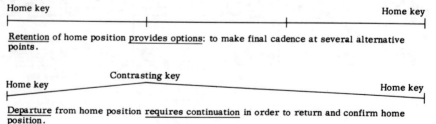

Home key   Home key

<u>Retention</u> of home position <u>provides options</u>: to make final cadence at several alternative points.

                         Contrasting key
Home key   Home key

<u>Departure</u> from home position <u>requires continuation</u> in order to return and confirm home position.

This structural power of modulation, its ability to outline the contour of a large-scale form, is its most important role in Western music. Shifts of key lead the harmonic action continuously from one point of reference to another; they provide freshness and interest by contrasts of key color and settle the action firmly at the end by confirming the original key in a conclusive manner. Modulation provides the blueprints for the entire structure of a composition, be it fugue, minuet, sonata, concerto, or other form, small or large. Two examples of harmonic layouts are given below:

	Major—Mozart: Prague *Symphony, finale, measures*	*Minor—Beethoven: Quartet in C minor, Op. 18, no. 4, first movement, measures*
Tonic	1–30 (D major)	1–25 (C minor)
Shift to second key	31–63	26–33
Second key	63–151 (A major)	34–74 (E♭ major)
Shifting keys	152–215	75–135
Tonic key	216–349	136–219

By determining the key layout of a composition you will acquire a perspective of its structure that will enable you to fit all the details of harmonic action into place. Moreover, you should be able to sense very strongly how the harmonic drive toward points of arrival and confirmation fuses all the action within the piece into a continuous dynamic flow. In this way we no longer hear a piece as a section-to-section patchwork but rather as the embodiment of a large-scale tour of action.

In modulation, we are generally made aware of the new key by some kind of cadential action. Reduced to the barest essentials this means that some kind of tritone effect, proper to the new key, is introduced and expanded. Specifically, we change tones of the old key to create tritones of the new key, as follows:

EX. 6.   Creation of new tritones

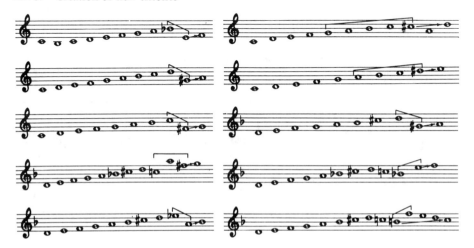

The entire scope of action in the examples given above was very modest, and the effects were quite gentle. In modulation, as in other types of musical action, we are concerned not only with *what* takes place but also with *how* it takes place. The gentle shifts of tonal center in Ex. 6 were virtually identical to the subsidiary cadential action described in Chap. 20. Other types of modulation described had profound structural implications. In modulation, the range of effect can be very great. Here are three examples:

EX. 7.   Types of modulation, or shift of tonal center

In Ex. 7*a,* we hear the merest nuance, indicating for a brief instant a glance in the direction of the second tonal center. The flow of harmony in the original key was enriched, but the progression was no more than a subsidiary cadential formula. In Ex. 7*b,* we explore for a short time in the area of the second key, but we do not commit ourselves formally. The final point of arrival is the home key. Key contrast here was marked but not confirmed. In Ex. 7*c,* we accept a formal commitment to the new key. There is a broadly scaled harmonic movement away from the home key which culminates with an authentic cadence in the new key.

The first two examples *indicate* the second tonal center with various degrees of clarity or emphasis; the third *establishes* and *confirms* the second tonal center. These are the three degrees of emphasis with respect to shift of tonal center: (1) *indication,* which makes a gesture in the new direction; (2) *establishment,* which represents clear arrival at the new key and action within it; and (3) *confirmation,* which clinches the entire matter with final formal cadential action. (See Chap. 10, page 102.) In the *Prague* Symphony (see page 223) indication of the new key is clearly given at about measure 55, establishment takes place from measure 63 on, and confirmation is made from about measure 120 to the double bar.

While it is possible and often very striking to shift from a given key to any other key in the major-minor system, most modulations involve keys which are closely related in scale degrees (that is, key signature) to the home key. A balance between key contrast and smooth progression is achieved. For any major key, the closely related degrees are II (minor), III (minor), IV (major), V (major), VI (minor). These, as you can see, appear as triads within the home key. Likewise, a minor home key will invite modulation to its diatonically related degrees, these being III (major), IV (minor), V (minor) (sometimes major), VI (major), VII (major). In Ex. 8 these modulations are illustrated with establishment and confirmation of the new key in each case. (The phases of the cadential action are indicated by 1–4–7–1 in each key.)

EX. 8. Modulations to various degrees

Major

a. I–II

b. I–III

c. I–IV

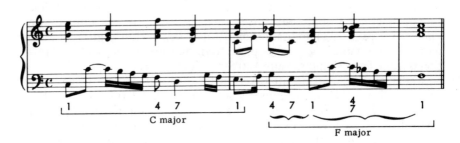

d. I–V

e. I–VI

Minor

f. I–III

g. I–IV

h. I–V

i. I–VI

j. I–VII

EX. 9.   Examples of modulation from music literature

a. I–III

Mendelssohn: *Songs without Words,* Op. 62, no. 1

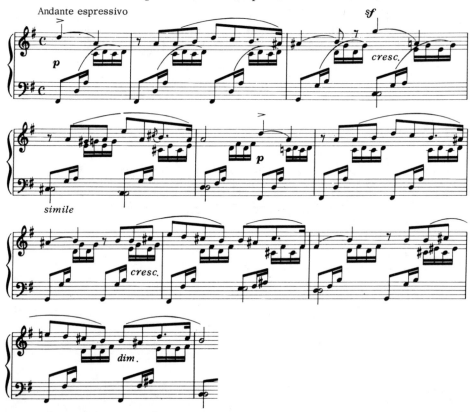

b. I–V in minor mode

Mozart: Sonata in A major, K. 331

c. I–IV

Schubert: Sonata in B♭, Scherzo

Allegro vivace con delicatezza

d. I–III in minor mode

Haydn: Sonata in D, finale

Presto, ma non troppo

By use of cadential formulas it is possible to construct a convincing modulation between any two keys and, indeed, at any point within a period. In the structural layouts of eighteenth- and early nineteenth-century music, however, the optimum structural balance is achieved when a firm arrival at the dominant in the case of major keys and the relative major in the case of minor keys is accomplished. In forms of considerable length, the shift from the first to the second key will occupy a group of periods, and the confirmation of the second key will actually require more time and effort than the establishment of the first key.

Within a normal or extended period which modulates, the first phrase is concerned with projecting the tonic feeling clearly. The second and whatever subsequent phrases are incorporated make the move to the second key, generally by a series of increasingly stronger cadential formulas. Composers have given a great deal of attention to ways in which such modulations may be made. They have sought for fresh, striking, and convincing paths to the new key. Timing has been a basic consideration. Some modulations involve a powerful drive to the new key, piling up momentum by means of a chain of cadential formulas; other modulations create surprise by sudden shift, by an early commitment which is then secured by strong cadential action. In line with the approach developed in this section of this text, we are presently concerned with structural aspects; later we shall look at the coloristic possibilities of shifting tonal centers.

Before we proceed to explore further the structural aspects of modulation, we should discuss briefly one idea that is generally included in the concept of modulation. That is the *pivot* chord.

Since modulation represents a change of direction, it would seem logical to suppose that there is a point at which the direction changes. Thus far, the change of direction has been indicated by the first cadential formula in the new key, and, indeed, we should never be sensible of a change in direction unless that new cadential formula were heard. Still, the intention of the composer to shift the tonal center may be in his mind *before* he arrives at the new cadential formula. He is writing in the *old* key, but he is beginning to think in the *new* key. Thus, he visualizes a *pivot* chord. This is a chord which stands in both keys, diatonically. The chord is ambivalent. It serves one function in the old key and another function in the new key. For example, VI in C major becomes IV in E minor, changing its function from *tonic* to *subdominant*. This and other pivot relationships are illustrated below:

EX. 10.   Pivot relationships

Diatonic pivot relationships add strength and smoothness to shifts of tonal center. However, they are by no means essential. The important process of modulation is the indication and establishment of the new key by cadential formulas.

SUMMARY

1. Modulation involves a formal shift of key, a commitment to another key by means of an authentic cadence.

2. A plan of modulation provides a basic structural layout for both small- and large-scale forms.

3. Modulation is generally accomplished by cadential action, involving the appearance of the tritone of the new key.

4. Shifts of tonal center may be made with the following degrees of strength:

 a. Implication, equivalent to secondary-dominant action

 b. Indication, internal section of a period momentarily in the second key with no strong cadence

 c. Establishment, clear commitment to the new key by continued action for a phrase or longer

 d. Confirmation, the new key formally secured by a strong authentic cadence, often by a series of authentic cadences creating an area of arrival

5. Modulations are possible between any two keys; in practice, the modulations to the dominant in major and to the relative major in minor keys provide the greatest structural strength.

6. In constructing a modulation a pivot chord, a chord which is diatonic in both keys, helps to provide a smooth path to the new key. It is by no means, however, necessary.

EXERCISES

1. Analyze excerpts from music literature for the techniques used in shifting tonal center. Pay particular attention to the relationship of the keys involved, the method used to reach the new key, and the length of the modulatory passage.

2. Identify by ear from dictation modulations to various degrees from a given tonic.

3. Write periods in which a transitory modulation takes place but in which the final cadence is in the home key.

4. Write periods in which a formal, confirmed modulation is made and which ends with a firm area of arrival in the new key.

5. Starting in a given key, with a specified opening figure, modulate to the closely related degrees of the home key, as in Ex. 8.

Chapter Twenty-two

Two-reprise Form

The materials and procedures we have been studying have represented the style of the eighteenth and early nineteenth centuries in music. These elements are worked together to achieve a level of structural completeness in countless small compositions based upon song and dance styles. Most of these small pieces are organized in what was described by musical theorists of the time as *two-reprise* form.

The term *reprise* signifies a repeat sign in general musical terms of the present day. It also signified, in the eighteenth century, that section of a composition which was enclosed by repeat marks. Thus, the two-reprise form consisted of a composition in which there were two sections, each marked off and distinguished from each other by being repeated.

The origin of the two-reprise form lies very probably in medieval antiquity, if not earlier. Dances and poetry were accompanied by music; the balance and symmetry of dance patterns and poetic lines were reflected in musical structures which consisted of two complementary phrases or periods. Often, the first phrase or period ended with some sense of incompleteness or digression. The second phrase or period rounded off the form with a close that gave a sense of return or completion. In early dances and songs the music was straightforward, rather simple in manner, generally without much elaboration; this simplicity of style befitted the role of music as background or support for songs and dances.

During the eighteenth century dance and song music was constantly being used as source material for independent musical compositions. From a straightforward, small-scale type of model the music tended to grow in scope and complexity. Often a composer would begin a piece as a dance or song, establishing the impression of the particular style firmly. Then when the listener would be thoroughly settled and comfortable in the manner of the piece, the composer would introduce striking digressions, imbalances, and extensions, to make a much bigger piece than would have been suspected at first. Periodically, he would return to the symmetrical dance manner in order to provide an area of orientation, of relaxation and arrival. The two-reprise form accommodated both the small- and large-scale plans of action.

There was no sharp line of distinction between the two kinds of musical action, the symmetrical dance on the one hand and the extension on the other. Extensions crept into dance music almost unnoticed when the music was written for listening and not for dancing. First, we shall write pieces that retain the structural regularity of true dance music. Still, even within this small scope we can ·impart some richness of content in melody and texture that can intrigue the listener. Later we shall undertake some expansions.

LAYOUTS OF THE TWO-REPRISE FORM

In all forms consisting of two reprises, or *parts,* the overall structural plan is as follows:

1. The first section establishes a musical point of departure and ends in such a manner as to convey something of incompleteness or digression.
2. The second section is concerned with a feeling of return and undertakes to create a complete sense of finality at its conclusion.

The basic plan may be diagrammed as follows:

EX. 1.   Overall plan of two-reprise form

In earlier times, dance music organized in the manner outlined above was said to have an *ouvert* (open ending) in the first section and a *clos* (closed ending) in the second section. All musical forms, large or small, which are derived from this two-part plan carry out, on their largest dimensions, this cycle of departure to a nonfinal point of arrival and return to a final point of arrival.

In music of the eighteenth and nineteenth centuries this plan is most characteristically and frequently embodied in compositions that ranged in scope from the smallest dances to the most highly extended and elaborate sonata and symphony movements. The internal arrangement of keys and melodic material among two-reprise forms indicates such a range of options that we must conclude that the only fixed conditions were those set forth in the diagram of Ex. 1.

Still, we can point to several general types of layout which we shall list below. Since the style in which these forms were composed is one which requires some sort of adequate balance between statements and counterstatements, an inner symmetry, it is likely that we shall find that the plan of reprise I will have some control over the structure of reprise II; this applies especially to the length of reprise II, which is as long as, or longer than, reprise I but never shorter. The following options are common to two-reprise forms:

Reprise I

1. Period ending with full cadence in I
2. Period ending with half cadence on V of tonic key
3. Period modulating to dominant with authentic cadence in V
4. Group of periods, two or more, the first centered upon the tonic key, the subsequent periods then modulating to the dominant with a strong cadential confirmation to end the first reprise

Reprise II

1. A phrase ending on a half cadence in the home key, followed by a phrase closing reprise II with an authentic cadence in the home key
2. A phrase ending on a half cadence in the home key, followed by a full restatement of the period comprising reprise I ending with an authentic cadence in the home key
3. A group of phrases, or perhaps several periods, ending upon a broad half cadence in the home key, possibly with dominant extensions or pedal points; restatement of all of reprise I modified harmonically to close upon the tonic with a broad authentic cadence, possibly with some additional cadential material

Harmonically, by far the most preferred plan, the plan which reflects the dynamic and logical aspects of the style, is that in which the first reprise closes in the dominant while the second closes in the tonic. This we shall call the I–V—x–I plan. It is the basis of many dances, arias, and the large-scale structural plan generally known as sonata form.

As a guide to analysis and composition, we shall list some of the combinations which may be made between the options of reprise I and reprise II:

I	II
1	1 or 2
2	1 or 2 or 3
3	2 or 3, possibly 1
4	3

An example of a two-reprise form which does not shift key at all and represents the first option for each reprise is the theme for the variations in Mozart's A-major Sonata. Following are three examples of forms based upon the two-reprise layout. (It should be pointed out that at times the double bars are omitted; this does not, however, destroy the validity of describing such a form as having the general two-reprise plan.)

EX. 2.   Two-reprise forms

a. Mozart: Sonata in A major, K. 331, Rondo

Alla Turca
Allegretto (♩ = 126)

Reprise I option 3
Reprise II option 3

b. Schumann: *Songs for Children,* Op. 79, no. 10

Reprise signs not employed in this composition.

(*continued*)

Reprise I option 3
Reprise II option 1 (with final phrase repeated)

c. Bach: Chorale, *Es ist das Heil ins kommen her*

Reprise I option 3
Reprise II option 1 (with an additional phrase)

Despite differences in layout and stylistic detail, the three examples given above have certain basic features in common:

1. They all make a deliberate, formal shift of tonal center, secured at the end of reprise I.

2. They all pass through a phase of harmonic instability at the beginning of reprise II; the impression of the new key which we received at the end of reprise I is thus blurred, and we are prepared to accept the return of the home key, signaled by a half cadence.

3. They all close firmly in the home key.

For us, the most interesting part of the form at present is the phase of harmonic instability. We can sense a tighter, more intense quality of movement; here the melodic values are less salient, receding in favor of a somewhat exploratory harmonic feeling. Motives constitute the principal melodic interest, rather than a well-rounded tuneful phrase.

In reprise II, two kinds of harmonic action take place:

1. Some kind of harmonic instability generally follows directly after the cadence of reprise I. This may involve:
   a. Exploration in related keys.
   b. Active or unstable harmony within the home key.

2. After the phase of harmonic instability, harmonic action is directed to a strong half cadence.

In the following example a number of possibilities for harmonic layout are sketched. These are taken from eighteenth-century music.

EX. 3.   Harmonic sketches of reprise II

a. Mozart: Quintet in C major, K. 515, Menuetto

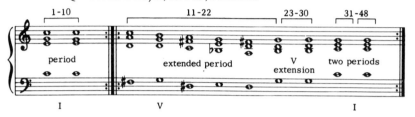

b. Haydn: Symphony No. 102 in B♭ major, Menuetto

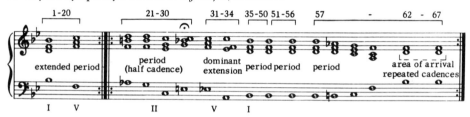

c. Beethoven: Sonata in D major, Op. 28, Scherzo

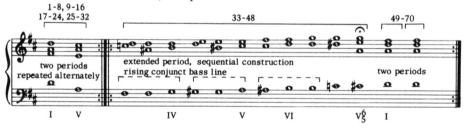

You will note that the progression in the first part of the second reprise has one clear harmonic direction; it drives forward to the dominant which makes the half cadence and prepares the return of the home key. Often we are not certain as to what exactly is taking place harmonically in the "x" section, but in retrospect, after we have arrived at the dominant, we can accept the logic of the harmonic progression which brought us to the dominant, and further, we can appreciate the composer's choice of the harmonic options available to him in the "x" section.

Melodic layout in two-reprise forms tends to concentrate upon one well-defined, fully evolved idea, rather than upon a tight play of short motives. A "tuneful" quality is highly appropriate for such small yet complete forms. The following is a standard layout for forms which are made up with two periods which are more or less equal in length.

Reprise I

Phrase I. Statement of melodic idea.

Phrase II. Counterstatement by varied repetition or mild contrast. (This plan is identical with the normal eight-measure-period plan discussed in Chap. 10.)

Reprise II

Phrase I. Play on motives from the first period, or introduction of contrasted material consistent with general style of piece.

Phrase II. Restatement of phrase I or II from first period adjusted for final cadence in home key; or related material which has a cadential quality.

The two examples which follow represent this version of the two-reprise plan:

EX. 4.   Melodic layouts for two-reprise forms

a. Mozart: Sonata in C major, K. 330, second movement

b. Mozart: Sonata in D major, K. 576, second movement

Principal melodic idea

Adagio (♩ = 92)

fp *fp*

Phrase I

varied repetition

fp *fp* *fp*

cadence in I

Phrase II

contrasted material

mf *f*

Phrase III Harmony centers on V.

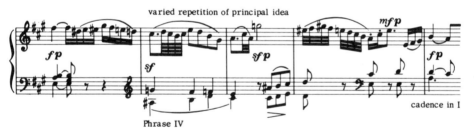

varied repetition of principal idea

mfp

fp *sf* *sfp* *fp*

cadence in I

Phrase IV

Project I. Sixteen-measure two-reprise forms, using dance styles such as minuet, gavotte, sarabande, bourrée, or march or song manner. Use the following layout:

1. Similar melodic material in both phrases of reprise I.
2. Half cadence in the fourth measure.
3. Full cadence in the dominant (or relative major, if the piece is in minor) at measure 8.
4. Varied or contrasted melodic material in measures 9–12. Arrange the motivic material sequentially.
5. Touch on II or VI preceded by their own dominants before making the half cadence at measure 12.
6. Restate the second phrase of reprise I with cadence adjusted for a close in the home key, measures 13–16; or use related material to bring out a satisfactory cadential feeling.

The periods you have already composed can serve very possibly as the first reprise in a form such as we have described above. If there is a modulation to the dominant in your period, no change need be made; if there is no such modulation, you should modify the harmonic progression so as to make an authentic cadence in the dominant. Modification, elaboration, and refinement of previous material is an excellent way to sharpen your skills and insights in musical composition. It enables you to know your material better, to develop elegance of style, and it carries out the approach to composition which is one of the fundamental aspects of eighteenth-century style and form, i.e., the modification and elaboration of previously available materials and models.

Project II. This project differs from Project I only in that reprise II is built somewhat differently. Instead of a single phrase optionally drawn from preceding material, following the half cadence in measure 12, we hear a full restatement of period I, with an adjustment for a cadence in the tonic key. Indeed, you can easily modify one of the examples of Project I to satisfy the conditions described for Project II.

There is, however, a significant difference in the melodic layout as the listener hears it when a full restatement of reprise I appears. We hear:

A, the principal melodic period or periods.
B, contrasted or intervening material.
A, return to the first melodic material.

This we make out quite easily as a *three-part form;* indeed, some theorists prefer to make a sharp distinction between a two-reprise form such as Ex. 4*a,* in which there is no well-defined melodic return, and a two-reprise form such as the following example. The first they designate as *two-part form;* the latter, as a *three-part form.*

EX. 5.   Three-part melodic structure in two-reprise form

Haydn: Sonata in D major, finale

The question concerning the greater validity or accuracy of the two-part or the three-part analysis, i.e., which is more basic or which reflects more faithfully the structural organization of the music—this question becomes still more critical when the two-reprise form is expanded. The author of this book will state his position in this question in the final sections of the present chapter.

EXPANSION OF TWO-REPRISE FORM

Perhaps, as you were working out the structure of the pieces assigned in Projects I and II, you may have felt that the sixteen- or twenty-measure blueprint was constrictive. Perhaps a phrase called for an extra pair of measures or so, or the final cadence would have been more impressive had it been broadened somewhat. Unless the musical material is originally utterly clear in its symmetry or made so by drastic simplification, the full cycle of musical action may be curtailed by a mechanical symmetry. This reflects a tendency toward expansion; it is generated by the need to give fuller scope to musical momentum. Such tendencies are to be observed in all kinds of music from every period since medieval times. Composers of the eighteenth and nineteenth centuries put this tendency to work very effectively in the two-reprise form; likewise, we shall undertake to expand this form.

We have already worked out some extended periods. The techniques we applied at that time can operate very effectively in the present case. Thus, at the end of either reprise I or II we can create extensions by:

1. Deceptive cadences.
2. Lightened authentic cadences.
3. Melodic or rhythmic action at the cadence point, leading beyond that point.
4. Expansion of the area of arrival by a series of cadential formulas.

Extensions at the end of part I call for much the same kind of extensions at the end of part II, *with the same melodic material*. Thus, any gesture toward expansion in the first part of the form serves double duty from a structural point of view. This is especially true in the classic style which is based upon a clear relationship between statement and counterstatement.

In the "x" section, there are several opportunities for expansion, as listed below:

1. We can expand the digression section. The first four or six measures can carry out some pattern of modulation in sequential or exploratory fashion; at a

convenient point we may linger for a short time upon one harmony or within some related tonal center. If we do this, it will probably require four to eight measures or more to make our way back to the dominant.

    2. The dominant which leads to a return of the home key can effectively be prolonged. A dominant pedal point or some other technique for dominant prolongation, such as we have covered in Chap. 20, can be used to carry out this procedure.

    In the following example from the D major Quartet of Mozart, K. 575, the measure count for the standard minuet form would be sixteen or thirty-two measures. By means of extensions, Mozart raised the count to seventy-four and, much more important, created a piece with heightened musical interest, one that grew by virtue of the contrast between the symmetrical dance style and skillfully introduced imbalances.

EX. 6.   Mozart: Quartet in D major, K. 575, Menuetto

Reprise I

expansion of dominant; new melodic material

area of arrival and confirmation of dominant

Reprise II

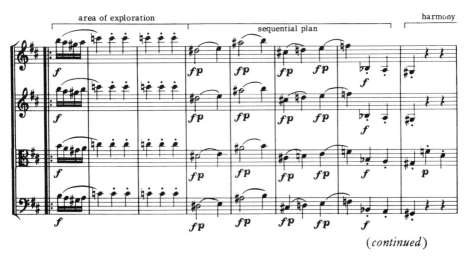

(continued)

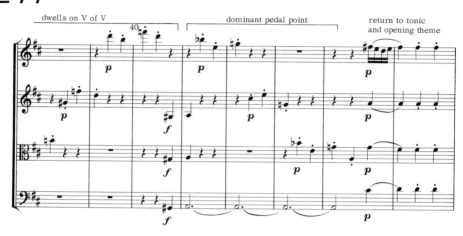

restatement of second period of Part I in home key

final area of arrival in tonic; repeated authentic cadences

added measure

You have no doubt noted that the melodic material which ended reprise II was a transposed version of the end of reprise I. The material was the same; the harmonic meaning was different. This correspondence of material with a change of harmonic meaning is a broadly scaled musical rhyme that provides a long-range melodic-harmonic statement-and-counterstatement relation within the form and helps to bind the piece into a rounded structure. This occurs in many two-reprise forms and is absolutely typical of classical sonata form. When we hear material stated in the home key that was originally presented in the dominant, we have one more sign that the supremacy of the tonic has been confirmed and that the harmonic books of the form have been balanced.

In this minuet, we can see the music taking on some substantial form. Suppose, then, if instead of writing a period for each stage of the operation, we were to create three or four, perhaps more. We should then arrive at a structure perhaps two or three hundred measures in length. This would be equivalent, both in length and in harmonic layout, to the sonata form of the classical style. As the phases of movement expand, the richness of content, the scope of digression, and the intensity of gesture will increase accordingly. This we do not propose to do here. Still, by looking at large-scale classical form in this way, we can get a better understanding of what is taking place at any point in a composition. We can appreciate the massive structure established by the harmonic action in the background, while, at the same time, we can relish the fascinating details of melody, textural play, and stylistic nuance, all in relation to the grand plan.

TWO-PART VERSUS THREE-PART FORM

It was indicated in the discussion concerning Project II that the melodic layout of some two-reprise forms is in three parts. The question of two- versus three-part form is more basic than the matter of melodic arrange- ment. It reaches the point at which we should decide whether such forms are fundamentally bipartite or tripartite in structure; that is to say, do we establish, as the first criterion of structural analysis, a two-part or three- part arrangement? The points in favor of a three-part arrangement may be listed as follows:

1. The A–B–A melodic layout when reprise I is restated
2. The solid return to the tonic in the second reprise which tends to suggest that what follows this return may be a third part
3. The proportions of the melodic layout which establish a symmetry of rela- tively equal parts as in Ex. 2a

The three-part arrangement according to these points is rather clear in its profile and very easily grasped by the listener.

The points in favor of a two-part arrangement are:

1. All such forms grew from, and are options of, a two-reprise form which is essentially two-part in its layout.
2. The I–V—x–I plan is essentially a two-part cycle of action, in which the final cadences balance each other.
3. The autonomy of the two reprises, in that each may be repeated in suc- cession, defines a two-part division.

According to these points, the two-part arrangement is less easy for the listener to discern. It is not a graphically clear layout; rather, it is a gener- ating premise which gives rise to many different options included among which may be a three-part melodic plan.

It is possible to account for the discrepancies in the relative lengths of parts I and II through an explanation of the harmonic action of the I–V— x–I plan.

From a harmonic point of view, the *establishment* of the tonic and its *supplantation* by the dominant is a double action, counterbalanced by the double action of *exploration* and *reestablishment* of the tonic. That the latter actions take longer and involve more effort is only logical in view of the basic sense of compensation between movement and arrival, stability and instability in music of this style. The strongest key impression we receive is that of the tonic at the beginning. To overcome this and replace the tonic by the dominant requires greater time and effort, just as repair or replacement requires often more than initial construction. Reasoning along the same lines, the subsequent actions, exploration and reestablishment, each require extended efforts in order to accomplish the double purpose of erasing the effect of previous action and confirming its own action. If we listen harmonically and rhythmically, we cannot fail to sense the two-part articulation of this process, where the heavier weight of the first part requires a compensating leverage of greater length in the second part. The diagram below illustrates this relationship graphically:

EX. 7.   Relative harmonic weights of reprises I and II

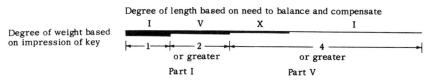

The interlocking and overlapping relationship of three-part melodic structure and two-part harmonic-rhythmic structure gives this form an organic tightness that is totally convincing, and at the same time the ambiguity provides the composer with innumerable alternatives with respect to melodic and harmonic action, so much so that this basic layout is the form par excellence of much baroque music, most classical music, and a great deal of romantic music.

Hence, when we compose or observe a two-reprise form, we shall be on the more solid ground if we visualize it as being generated out of a two-cycle plan of action, the second of which can be expanded to create a three-part melodic layout *without* destroying the compensating action which reprise II provides against reprise I.

(*Note:* In his book, *Music—The Listener's Art,* McGraw-Hill, 1957, the author discusses the question of two-part versus three-part form, pp. 177–180. The preference for the two-part interpretation is in line with the position of eighteenth-century theorists and such modern critics as Tovey. In this present chapter, there is one modification of the view taken in the preceding book. That is the substitution of the term *reprise* for the term *part* in designating the form. Technically, this is a more exact description of the forms considered in this chapter, although writers of the eighteenth century used both *reprise* and *part* in describing the form.)

Project III. Expand one of the shorter forms previously composed in Project I or II employing the following procedures:

1. Extend reprise I in one or more of the following ways:
   a. Deceptive cadence at measure 8, followed by a strong authentic cadence by way of compensation in the second key.
   b. Period or phrase using new or related material, following the cadence in the new key. This period should be entirely in the new key.
   c. Cadential formulas in the second key to create an area of arrival.
2. Extend reprise II in one or more of the following ways:

a. Eight or more measures of unstable harmony using (1) circle of fifths with secondary dominants; (2) pedal point on the dominant
b. Cadential formulas emphasizing dominant preparation for return to tonic
c. Restatement of material of reprise I with adjustment of harmony so that *b* and *c* of reprise I are set in the home key
d. Extension of *c* possibly with a tonic pedal point

Analyze minuets and other two-reprise forms to determine how the procedures listed above are handled in each individual situation.

Chapter Twenty-three

Interchange of Mode

When we studied the minor mode, we learned that it acquired its cadential function by borrowing the leading tone from the major mode on the same degree. In this way, a minor mode could stand as a tonal center with a strength nearly equal to that of the major mode. 1, 4, and raised 7 in minor are identical with 1, 4, and 7 of the major mode.

This parallelism of degree and function between major and minor modes on the same degree has given rise to *interchange of mode*. Briefly, this means that it is possible to *switch* modes while retaining the same tonal center. The implications of interchange of mode for eighteenth- and nineteenth-century music are tremendous. Both harmonic structure and harmonic color are involved.

In most instances, the minor mode is introduced in a major-mode composition, after the feeling for major has been firmly established. Consider how this expands the area of keys related to any given major mode. We have, for example:

EX. 1. Diagram of keys related through interchange of mode

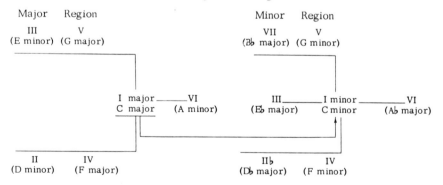

Structurally, interchange of mode is strongly bound up with expansion, as the following example shows:

EX. 2.   Expanded period structure with interchange of mode

a. Mozart: "Sonata" in F major, K. 533, second movement

b. Beethoven: Concerto for Violin in D major, Op. 61, first movement

Harmonic color too is involved when two major keys, very different in sound from each other but related by interchange of mode, are placed in juxtaposition to each other, as in the following example:

EX. 3. Coloristic effect in interchange of mode

Schubert: Quintet in C major, Op. 163, first movement

An inflected tone borrowed for an instant from the minor mode adds a nuance of more intense or poignant expression to the major quality; it "sweetens" the major mode by contrast.

EX. 4.   Major mode colored by inflection borrowed from minor mode

Schubert: Quintet in C major, Op. 163, first movement

From the examples given above, we can see that interchange of mode ranges in effect from the slightest nuance to very broad structural elaborations. When we consider the specific techniques involved in interchange of mode we shall be concerned with two matters:

1. The kind of chord used
2. The structural value of the interchange

Interchange of mode is bound up with cadential action, especially in the classical style. Therefore, we shall classify the chords used in this procedure according to their cadential functions in a *major* key.

1. Subdominant-function chords
a. Minor subdominant
b. II with lowered fifth
c. II⁷ with lowered fifth
d. Neapolitan sixth chord
2. Tonic-function chords
a. Minor tonic
b. VI with lowered root and fifth
3. Chords of the augmented sixth
a. Six-three
b. Six-five-three
c. Six-four-three
4. Dominant-function chords
a. Diminished seventh
b. Minor ninth chord
c. III with lowered root

Structurally, interchange of mode has the following functions:

1. Coloration of the subdominant stage of a cadential formula, often with no more than a single tone or chord

2. Shift between tonic major and minor within a motive or phrase, again used for coloristic purposes

3. Shift between interchange-related keys within a motive or phrase, for purposes of harmonic color

4. Extension of a period by digression to minor-mode area or by means of a deceptive cadence in the minor mode

5. Modulation, often to dramatize the formal shift from tonic to dominant

6. As a resource in the "x" section of a two-reprise form

7. Participation in dominant extensions and pedal points

First we shall explain each chord and then examine ways in which interchange may be used structurally.

SUBDOMINANT-FUNCTION CHORDS

1. *Minor subdominant.* This chord may take its place in a typical cadential formula. It also may alternate effectively with the tonic chord. In a cadential formula the minor subdominant may be preceded by tonic harmony, by its own dominant, or by the major version of the subdominant chord. Minor subdominant harmony proceeds effectively to dominant, cadential $^6_4$, or a chord on the raised fourth degree, either diminished triad or diminished seventh. It may also be used in a plagal cadence.

EX. 5.   Uses of the minor subdominant triad

a. Mozart: Sonata in B♭ major, K. 333, first movement

b. Schubert: Quintet in C major, Op. 163, finale

254

c. Schubert: Quintet in C major, Op. 163, second movement

In Ex. 5*g* note the effectiveness of the progression from the lowered sixth degree to the dominant in the first inversion of the minor subdominant. This half-step progression is a leading-tone action in reverse; it carries considerable historical and stylistic significance. The progression marked in brackets is a version of the Phrygian cadence (see Chap. 19). Later on we shall learn to use an elaborated version of the Phrygian cadence often discovered in eighteenth- and nineteenth-century music. Contemporary music frequently takes advantage of the cadential effect of the Phrygian progression, giving focus and clarity to tone groups that would otherwise be obscure in their harmonic meaning. This we can find in the music of Bartók and Hindemith especially.

2. *II with lowered fifth.* This chord is typically part of a cadential formula. In more than three voices the middle tone, the subdominant, is doubled.

EX. 6. II with lowered fifth

3. *II⁷ with lowered fifth.* Like the II triad with lowered fifth, this chord is best used in a cadential formula, preferably as part of a broad authentic cadence. The seventh is prepared and resolved in the usual way. I, IV, and IV♭³ may be used to approach II ♭⁵ and II ♭ ⁷ 5.

EX. 7.   II⁷ with lowered fifth

Mozart: Quartet in C major, K. 465, second movement

4. *The Neapolitan sixth chord*. This chord, which we became acquainted
with in Chap. 19, adds a very striking note of color when used in the major
mode as the representative of subdominant harmony. Like the minor subdominant, this chord may be used by itself or in connection with a phrase
in the minor-mode area. Frequently, the Neapolitan sixth chord provides
the link between a phrase in the minor mode and the authentic cadence
in the major mode which ends the period.

EX. 8. Neapolitan sixth in major mode

a. Mozart: Quartet in C major, K. 465, finale

b. Schubert: Quintet in C major, Op. 163, first movement

The Neapolitan sixth chord can be preceded by any of the following harmonies:

1. Tonic, moving to the N⁶ as a dominant resolving deceptively to its own VI with lowered root and fifth
2. Dominant of IV moving to N⁶ in same manner as above
3. Dominant or dominant seventh of the N⁶ proceeding directly from tonic or from minor-mode harmony
4. Minor subdominant

EX. 9. Approach to Neapolitan sixth in interchange of mode

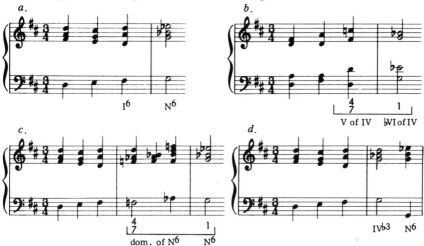

The Neapolitan sixth proceeds as one might expect a chord of subdominant function to act. Following are some options:

1. Directly to dominant harmony
2. To the cadential $^6_4$ chord
3. To the diminished triad or diminished seventh on the raised fourth degree

These are illustrated below:

EX. 10. Progression following the Neapolitan sixth chord in interchange of mode

In extended periods the Neapolitan area (♭ second degree) can be expanded with its own constellation of cadential formulas, thus constituting an important section within the period. This is illustrated in Ex. 8*a*. Note the

broad cadence which returns the harmony to the home key, measures 318–326.

When we use minor-subdominant-function harmony in the cadential system of harmony, we can treat it simply as an inflection or as a broadly scaled gesture. Minor subdominant harmony does not necessarily disturb the major quality of a period.

When we use minor tonic harmony within the classic cadential system of harmony, the structural implications are much greater. The minor third changes the essential character of the tonic triad and indeed of the key feeling itself. It tends to undermine the stability of the major harmony and, in doing so, can be turned to extremely effective use in building structure on a broad scale.

TONIC-FUNCTION CHORDS

1. *Tonic minor.* In the classical system of tonality, the tonic minor chord exerts the most wide-reaching effect when it is introduced into major; it has a much greater significance than minor chords of subdominant or dominant function in so far as structure is concerned. The tonic minor is characteristically introduced at a critical cadential point. This may be at the culmination of an authentic cadence or following a half cadence. Following are some sketches of compositions which make use of the tonic minor in this way:

EX. 11.   Sketches of structural use of tonic minor

a. Haydn: Symphony No. 102 in Bb major, finale

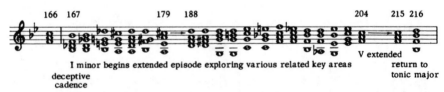

b. Mozart: Quintet in D major, K. 593, first movement

c. Mozart: Quartet in A major, K. 464, first movement

d. Beethoven: Quartet in F major, Op. 59, no. 1, first movement

digression within extended period

change of scale to
minor mode within period

As the sketches above indicate, the tonic minor may be used to extend a period within the home key, or it may be used to initiate a modulation to the dominant key. In both cases, an entire set of progressions in the minor-key area, involving a number of cadential formulas, must be worked out in order to give the proper scope to the action started with the tonic minor chord.

When the tonic minor follows a half cadence, the most effective way of highlighting the change in mode is to restate the opening material of the preceding phrase verbatim, except for change of mode. This is demonstrated in the following example:

EX. 12.   Parallel melodic construction with interchange of mode

Mozart: Sonata in F major, K. 332, second movement

When the tonic minor is used at the end of a period, new melodic material may be introduced effectively. This gives the impression of an episode or digression, dramatized by new melodic material, as below:

EX. 13.   Tonic minor with new material at end of period

Mozart: Sonata in F major, K. 332, finale

Starting with Beethoven and Schubert, nineteenth-century composers used the tonic minor in opposition to the major as an effect of chiaroscuro. This coloristic device need not have any structural effect upon a period. However, it introduces a color value that invites later reappearance. Here is an example:

EX. 14. Tonic minor used coloristically

Schubert: Impromptu in C major

2. *VI with lowered root and fifth.* This chord is characteristically used in a deceptive-cadence situation, as in Ex. 2*b*. Such deceptive cadences appear where a period in a major key would normally end, and the material used can well be contrasted to the previous melodic material, also as in Ex. 2*b*. It is also possible to use VI♭ within a period as a means of achieving expanded structure through digression, as in the following example:

EX. 15. VI♭ used within a period

Beethoven: Quartet in D major, Op. 18, no. 3, finale

(*continued*)

VI♭ is most strikingly approached by the dominant or dominant seventh of the major key. However, it can be reached smoothly by sideslipping from tonic major or minor, as follows:

EX. 16.   Approach to VI♭

Schubert: Quintet in C major, Op. 163, first movement

CHORDS OF THE AUGMENTED SIXTH

In the following progression, we hear a cadential formula involving minor subdominant to dominant. The minor subdominant is in the first inversion. This is a very familiar progression in traditional harmony, particularly in the positions indicated for the various voices. There is a strong temptation for the uppermost voice to ornament the progression from 4 to 5; a chromatic passing tone slips in very smoothly, as below:

EX. 17. Cadential fromula in minor and ornamentation thereof

In music of the sixteenth and seventeenth centuries, this progression was considered to be an ornamentation. In the eighteenth century, the chord marked at "x" in Ex. 17 became fixed through usage as an independent harmonic construction called the *chord of the augmented sixth*.

Originally, we find this elaboration taking place in Phrygian-mode harmony, as an enrichment of one of the Phrygian cadences. (The progression marked off in brackets is identical with a familiar Phrygian cadence.) Later, the augmented sixth chord became a resource in tonal harmony, as an approach to the authentic cadence.

The history of the augmented sixth chord tells us that the chord is not entirely arrived at in the manner of triads or seventh chords, that is, by combinations or superimpositions of thirds and fifths. Rather, it has come into harmonic practice ambiguously, as a combination of functional chord structure and melodic action.

The most familiar position of this chord is the one shown above, on the flat sixth degree of a major or minor key. As we hear the chord, we may be aware of an ambiguity of sound and of meaning. The combination of tones—A♭–C–F♯—sounds exactly like the dominant seventh of D♭ major—A♭–C–G♭. If we take the combination as an augmented sixth chord, it will resolve with each tone acting as a leading tone, C and F♯ resolving outward as members of the augmented fourth tritone, while A♭ moves downward as the lower member of the augmented sixth. Interpreted this way the chord has a relation to C minor–C major. As a dominant of D♭ major, G♭ and C will act as leading tones, closing in properly in the resolution of the diminished fifth, while A♭, a stable, firm tone in the bass, will drop to Db. The former resolution has a surprise value, changing the entire meaning of the harmony, while the latter resolution carries out the expectation of a sturdy confirmation of an indicated tonic chord.

EX. 18. Augmented sixth and dominant seventh ambiguity (between F and E)

Schubert: Quintet in C major, Op. 163, second movement

This double meaning of the augmented sixth—dominant seventh sound enables the chord to create an effective link between an episode in a minor-mode area and a final cadence in the parallel major. Here are some examples, reduced from a number of compositions:

EX. 19. Link between major and minor by means of augmented sixth chord (see Ex. 8*a*, measure 323, and Ex. 23, measure 310)

a. Mozart: Quintet in C major, K. 515, first movement

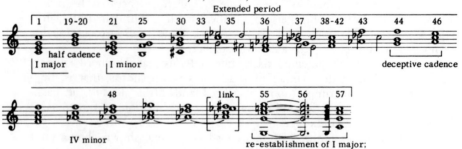

b. Schubert: Sonata in Bb major, first movement

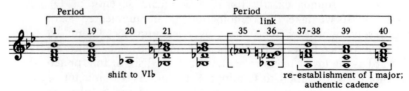

In the above examples we observe one of the traditional roles of the augmented sixth chord, that is, to form a passageway between remote tonal centers. Another important function of the chord is to reinforce the drive to a dominant chord, as in Ex. 17. In the nineteenth century chords of the augmented sixth were often used for special coloristic purposes.

The augmented ⁶₃ chord is the oldest and most common version of the three kinds of augmented sixth chords. Usually, the ⁶₃ appears with the augmented sixth in the outer voices. However, the two upper members of the chord may be inverted, depending upon the convenience of texture and part writing.

EX. 20.   Positions of the augmented ⁶₃ chord

a. Mozart: Sonata in E♭, K. 282, first movement

b. Beethoven: Symphony No. 5, Op. 67, first movement

In Ex. 20*c,* the chord is treated as having a diminished third. The effect of this position is not so bold and clear as in the augmented sixth position. Still, this diminished third position has been used with striking effect many times, where voice leading or expressive intention may have called for it.

In four-voice texture the ⁶₃ calls for the doubling of one tone. This must necessarily be 3, because of the obligations which the tones of the augmented sixth interval have with respect to resolution. Since each of these tones *must* move outward by half step, doubling either would create parallel octaves. Example 21 shows the chord in four voices, with several possible resolutions.

EX. 21.   Five resolutions of augmented ⁶₃ using four-part harmony

In the examples given above, note how the augmented $^6_3$ is approached: from minor IV, from VI, from minor I, from II with lowered root and fifth, and from the dominant itself. This last version is very effective when combined with a suspension over the raised fourth degree.

In the augmented $^6_3$ there is a gap between 3 and 6. This gap can be filled in several ways, giving rise to two other useful versions of the augmented sixth chord, the augmented $^6_5$ and augmented $^6_4$ as illustrated below:

EX. 22.   Augmented $^6_5$ and augmented $^6_4$

Each of these chords has a distinctive quality of sound. The $^6_5$ is identical in sound with a full dominant seventh, taking on firmness through the presence of the perfect fifth. The ambiguity of the $^6_3$, relating to two different tonal centers, is retained in the $^6_5$. The $^6_4$ sounds quite a bit more unstable than either of the two other versions. It actually relates to no familiar tonal center, being found in no major or minor scale. Its particular quality is derived from its two tritones and its two major thirds, which combine to create a peculiar saturation of dissonance. Each tone of the $^6_4$ dissonates against two other members of the chord.

Structurally, $^6_5$ and $^6_4$ are interchangeable with $^6_3$. They are used characteristically before the dominant in a cadential formula and may be approached by some version of tonic or subdominant harmony. However, since their coloristic aspects differ somewhat from those of the $^6_3$, they lend themselves to special treatment in certain situations.

In the case of $\frac{6}{5}$, its identity with the dominant seventh of the Neapolitan chord (the lowered II) enables us to approach it as if it truly were a dominant seventh chord. Hence, if we have arrived during an interchange-of-mode episode at either the Neapolitan chord or the triad on the flat sixth degree, we can proceed to the $\frac{6}{5}$ in the first case or add the minor seventh in the second case, creating the augmented $\frac{6}{5}$ chord. In such cases, a broad, grandly scaled cadence in the home key seems to be in order, and composers generally take advantage of this opportunity. They take the $\frac{6}{5}$ with its full dominant seventh sound to the cadential $\frac{6}{4}$ of the home key. In this manner an intensely dramatic and rich effect is created by the juxtaposition of these two unstable yet sonorous chords, chords which represent two highly contrasted qualities of harmonic color.

EX. 23. Augmented $\frac{6}{5}$ to cadential $\frac{6}{4}$, approached and resolved

Schubert: Quintet in C major, Op. 163, finale

(continued)

When $\frac{6}{3}$ moves to the cadential $\frac{6}{4}$, the voices proceed as follows:

♯4 moves to 5
♭6 moves to 5
1 remains on 1
♭3 moves to major 3

In the last item, ♭3 to major 3, the reestablishment of the major mode was confirmed. Many theorists complain that when the $\frac{6}{3}$ moves to the cadential major $\frac{6}{4}$, the chord is incorrectly notated. They recommend changing ♭3 to ♯2, so that a diatonic rather than a chromatic progression in this part will be created. The chord then is named the doubly augmented sixth. This interpretation loses sight entirely of the fact that an interchange of mode is taking place, and that the critical factor in this progression is the change from ♭3 to major 3, a truly chromatic progression. Therefore, the correct notation is ♭3, regardless of which chord follows.

Six-four-three, with its chromatic, highly unstable quality of sound, became valuable to nineteenth-century composers. We hear it often in the music of Richard Wagner, as, for example, within the first phrase of the Prelude to *Tristan und Isolde*. This chord is found from time to time in eighteenth-century music, preceding a dominant as an alteration of sub-dominant harmony. For example, if we take a $^6_3$ on the flat sixth degree and proceed chromatically as we have done before, we arrive at the augmented $^6_4{}_3$.

Following are several examples of the use of the augmented $^6_4{}_3$ chord. Some are entirely in the minor mode; others involve the interchange of mode.

EX. 24.   Uses of the augmented $^6_4{}_3$ chord

a. Mozart: Sonata in A minor, K. 310, first movement .

b. Schubert: Quintet in C major, Op. 163, finale

c. Beethoven: Quartet in F major, Op. 59, no. 1, third movement

Adagio molto e mesto

d. Beethoven: Sonata in C minor, Op. 13, finale

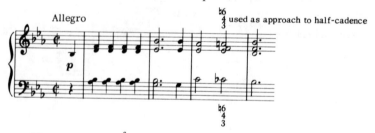

The augmented $\frac{6}{4}$ in Ex. 24*b* is an altered dominant seventh which uses the lowered second degree. The use in the Schubert Quintet represents a coloristic nuance within dominant-function harmony; indeed, the entire movement vacillates between C minor and C major, so that the final D♭ in the cadence acts to intensify the minor color previously heard.

Two of the examples given above illustrate some other characteristic uses of the augmented $\frac{6}{4}$, uses which can be applied also in the case of $\frac{6}{5}$, as well as $\frac{6}{3}$ and the tonic minor itself. The first of these is a descending chromatic bass line where the harmony touches upon the augmented sixth chord; the second is a dominant extension where the augmented sixth chord (or the minor tonic chord) alternates with dominant harmony.

Summarizing the augmented sixth chords:

1. They originate in the minor mode or the Phrygian mode.
2. Structurally they lead to dominant harmony.
3. The essential tones are ♭1, 3, and ♯6.
4. These chords have a variety of structural uses:
   a. They reinforce a half cadence.
   b. They strengthen an authentic cadence.
   c. They provide a link between minor-mode and major-mode areas.
   d. They link two remote key areas.

DOMINANT-FUNCTION CHORDS

These chords are most generally used to give a special inflection to dominant harmony in the major mode. They involve no special structural responsibility and may be used within a period or at a cadential point for color or emphasis. Examples of these chords are the diminished seventh and the dominant minor ninth; the augmented triad on the lowered third degree, while it may serve a dominant function, interchanging minor third for major, is rarely used in such a context.

EX. 25.   Dominant-function chords involving interchange of mode

a. Diminished seventh chord

Beethoven: Sonata in F minor, Op. 2, no. 1, second movement

b. Dominant minor ninth chord

Beethoven: Sonata in B♭, Op. 22

As we explained each chord in the major-minor interchange system, we gave some consideration to the structural implications of each chord. You may refer to the following compositions for additional examples of various types of usage:

1. *Subdominant coloration*

   Mozart: Quintet in E♭, K. 614, second movement, measure 18
   Beethoven: Quartet in G, Op. 18, no. 2, second movement, measures 83–85

2. *Shift between tonic major and minor*

   Beethoven: Sonata in C minor, Op. 13, finale, measures 30–37
   Mozart: Sonata in A minor, K. 310, finale, measures 29–32

3. *Extension of a period*

   Haydn: Symphony No. 103, finale, measures 121–130
   Beethoven: Quartet in F, Op. 59, no. 1, finale, measures 53–64

4. *Modulation*

   Beethoven: Quartet in G, Op. 18, no. 2, finale, measures 38–50
   Beethoven: Symphony No. 2 in D, first movement, measures 55–69

5. *Use in the "x" section of a two-part form*

   Haydn: Symphony No. 103, Menuetto, measures 11–31
   Beethoven: Symphony No. 2, Menuetto, measures 17–38

6. *Dominant extensions*

   Mozart: *Prague* Symphony, introduction, measures 28–36
   Beethoven: Symphony No. 3, Op. 55, first movement, measures 338–397

The usage described above does not by any means exhaust the possibilities of interchange of mode. Rather, we have explained here the main features of eighteenth- and early nineteenth-century procedure. With our consideration of the interchange of mode we have completed our study of classical, structurally organized harmony. We have endeavored to give harmony some genuine creative meaning by showing how it relates to rhythm, phrase and period structure, form, melody, texture, and general expressive value within the style period from which our most familiar musical idioms have been drawn. From the early nineteenth century on, continually greater interest has developed, and will continue to develop, in exploring harmony for fresh, new, and striking color. The principles of harmonic usage, however, have remained more or less as a guiding factor, and the relation of harmony to the other elements of music composition as explained here has been valid, though modified, down to the present day.

SUMMARY

1. Interchange of mode has both a coloristic and a structural aspect; the color aspect tends to be local in scope while the structural aspect is usually tied up with expansion of form.

2. In classical harmony interchange of mode is associated with cadential functions.

    a. Subdominant-function chords tend to emphasize a local color value.

    b. Dominant-function chords also provide the harmony with a local nuance.

    c. Tonic-function chords tend to open up the structure, leading to phrases and periods in remote flat-side keys; often modulations to the dominant are prepared by minor tonic harmony.

    d. Augmented sixth chords lead strongly to dominant harmony either on a local scale or as a link between minor-mode areas and the major key of the piece.

EXERCISES

1. Identify by listening the procedures of interchange of mode that are illustrated in the following passages:

Mendelssohn: *Songs without Words,* Op. 102, no. 5

Mozart: "Sonata" in F major, K. 533, first movement

Beethoven: Sonata in B♭ major, Op. 22, first movement

Mozart: Sonata in A major, K. 310, finale

2. Realize in four voices the basses given below. Include the following procedures and chords:

a. Minor subdominant (see page 253)

b. II$_{5b}^{7}$ (see page 255)

c. Neapolitan sixth (see page 256)

d. Minor tonic (see page 260)

e. VI♭ (see page 263)

f. $_{3}^{6\#}$ (see page 267)

g. $_{5b}^{6\#}$ (see page 268)

h. $_{4}^{6\#}$ (see page 271)

i. V^{9b} (see page 273)

j. VII^{7b} (see page 273)

k. Section of phrase in area of minor mode

3. Select a period previously composed; after the half cadence of the first phrase, shift into minor mode, build the period into an extended form, and (a) make a broad I$_{4}^{6}$—V^{7} cadence in the home major key; (b) make a broad modulation to the key of the dominant. (Two versions.)

4. Discover examples of interchange of mode in the music of Haydn, Mozart, Beethoven, and Schubert. Describe the process in each example, and indicate how the interchange process is associated with motivic, structural, and textural aspects.

5. Modify the two-reprise forms composed in connection with work for Chap. 22 so that the "x" section incorporates interchange of mode. If you wish, introduce elements of interchange of mode in reprise I and the latter part of reprise II.

Part Three

Harmonic Color

PREFACE

In describing the harmonic vocabulary and procedures covered in this text we have emphasized harmonic action. We have pointed out the ways in which the cadential formula and all its many variations and expansions have been directed to the organic, structurally firm embodiment of key. In the eighteenth century and in the early nineteenth century this role of harmony was of first importance in the minds of composers, performers, and listeners.

Still, the individual quality of each chord, the change of effect from chord to chord, the appeal of one texture compared to another, the striking color of alterations both in chords and in ornamental tones, the richness of effect in the minor mode, the brilliance of major harmonies—all these were part of the world of harmony in the eighteenth century. The element of color in harmony was exploited but only in relationship to the overall plan of action guided by the cadential formula.

It was inevitable that color would become increasingly important as composers sought to develop and enrich their sounds and textures. From the time of Bach, when color represented a shade and a nuance within a strongly directed exploration of the home-key area, to the time of Beethoven, when certain works, such as the *Pastorale* Symphony, seem to have arisen partly from the matrix of a certain color value, harmonic color more and more saturates the fabric of tonal harmony. After Beethoven, we can say that the balance slowly tips in favor of color and away from action until we reach the coloristic pointillism of musical impressionism.

As color values increase and the harmonic vocabulary becomes richer, the focus on a tonal center in terms of cadential harmony becomes less clear. While harmonic progressions recede from the area of diatonic tonality, voice leading which connects remotely related chords becomes much more important in the general scheme of composition. Melodic action, as we have seen in our previous work, can provide a binding action that adds considerable logic and vitality to musical movement. Eventually, in the late nineteenth and the twentieth centuries, composers relied heavily— in some cases, exclusively—upon linear action and melodic profile. In all the examples which will be used in the following chapters, you will find a significant factor of conjunct or strikingly disjunct voice leading which helps to organize the progressions. If we were to examine some progressions in the compositions of composers such as Richard Strauss, Scriabin, Bartók, or Hindemith, we should find combinations of sounds which are to a great extent justified by the fact that a number of voices happen to reach a certain set of pitches in their melodic progress.

In this book, we shall not proceed to so advanced a point. Wagner's style, the critical moment in the history of tonal harmony, represents for us the final station. Saturated as it is with chromaticism, it still retains the cadential logic and the traditional chord forms with which we have been concerned. While we shall pay due attention to the binding effect of linear action, we shall still use tonal functions as a basis of reference, since they represent the point from which most nineteenth-century chromaticism takes its departure.

Chapter Twenty-four

Chromatic Digressions
in Diatonic Harmony

In the following passages at the points marked "x" a single chord that is chromatic to the key is introduced:

EX. 1.   Chromatic chords in diatonic harmony

a. Schubert: Quintet in C major, Op. 163, first movement

(*continued*)

b. Wolf: *Grenzen der Menschheit*

Each of the chords marked produces a moment of coloristic harmonic inflection, a departure from the homogeneous quality of diatonic harmony. These chords seem to be used principally for their coloristic value, rather than for any functional purpose such as cadential action or formal modulation. In some cases, the color quality of the home key is thrown into sharper relief. Such harmonic effects can be likened to chiaroscuro or kaleidoscopic effects in pictorial representation.

We are not strangers to harmonic effects of contrasting colors. The minor mode, with its shifting degrees, and interchange of mode have provided resources of high color content. As we pointed out, however, whatever color values may have developed in these areas, they were all subordinated to the structural purposes of the harmony. We neither lingered overlong upon one striking sound, nor did we detach the special chord from its progression within a cadential formula.

In nineteenth-century music, both these processes, the extension of the sound and the loosening of the cadential connection, came to the fore. There is a marked tendency to seek out coloristic effects for their own immediate impact. Naturally, we shall find that musical structure is adapted to accommodate such effects. This does not necessarily mean an organic expansion; rather, it often entails a looser, more clearly sectionalized type of structure with a less insistent quality of movement. At times it is difficult to draw the line between the structural and the coloristic effects of a chord or phrase that embodies chromatic harmony; yet the direction in the nineteenth century is clearly toward color.

Since these inflections are often momentary, as in Ex. 1, we may incorporate them into the small structures with which we have been working. Still, a look at any large-scale work of the romantic period will provide many examples of the use of such inflections.

JUXTAPOSITION OF TRIADS

Two triads belonging to different scales can create a striking shift of harmonic color when they are sounded in succession. To our ears the most familiar and perhaps most pleasing effect of such juxtaposition occurs when we hear two major triads whose roots lie a major or minor third distant from each other. These are commonly called *third-related* progressions and are illustrated below:

EX. 2.   Third-related progressions

e. Mozart: Fantasia in C minor, K. 475

f. Brahms: Symphony No. 3 in F major, Op. 90, second movement

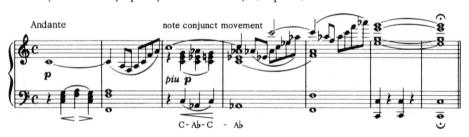

g. Dvorak: Symphony No. 5 in E minor, Op. 95

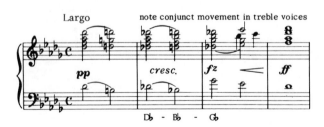

b. Schubert: Quintet in C major, Op. 163, first movement

i. Beethoven: Concerto for Piano in E♭, Op. 73, first movement

j. Brahms: Concerto for Violin in D, Op. 77, first movement

The examples given above and the excerpts from musical literature illustrate root movement between major triads upward and downward by major and by minor thirds. While the coloristic value is certainly the most prominent effect, it is important to note that these progressions often resemble or indeed replace procedures with which we are at present familiar. Thus, in Exs. 2e, 2h, measures 81 and 87, 2i, and 2j, the progressions are analogous to the resolution of the dominant after a half cadence. In 2f we hear a strong plagal effect, which is indeed secured by the minor subdominant. In 2g and 2h, measure 92, there is simply a coloristic juxtaposition of triads within or between phrases. In each case the effect is realized by a richly resonant texture.

Movement between major triads whose roots stand a third distant from each other is accomplished with a great deal of ease, since one tone is common to both chords, the other tones move by chromatic inflection, and only the bass need leap the third, if both chords are in root position. The more striking effects of color are achieved in root position or $^6_4$ position; $^6_3$ does not provide as clear or intense a quality of chord sound as the other positions.

Other types of chromatic triad juxtaposition may involve other root relationships than the third or may introduce minor triads. These will probably not sound as smooth as third-related major-triad progressions but may create a strikingly oblique quality of harmonic movement with a more pointed effect of harmonic emphasis. On the other hand, some of these progressions resemble portions of cadential formulas. Some examples of such progressions are given below:

EX. 3.   Juxtaposition of triads by seconds, augmented fourths; chromatic progressions involving minor triads

The major second root movement bears a strong resemblance to the sub-
dominant-dominant elements of the authentic cadence; the minor second
relationship harks back to the deceptive cadence of the minor mode while
the augmented fourth can be linked with the Neapolitan sixth–dominant
formula. However, if the context allows the listener to sense the progression as a tangential movement between two distantly related chords,
the cadential aspect is only implicit while the color aspect is salient. Some
examples from musical literature follow:

EX. 4.   Juxtaposition of triads by seconds, augmented fourths; chromatic progressions involving minor triads

a. Major triad on second degree as ornamental elaboration of cadence

Debussy: Preludes, Book I, no. 4

Permission for reprint granted by Durand et Cie, Paris, France, copyright owners;
Elkan-Vogel Co., Inc., Philadelphia, Pa., agents.

b. Major triad on lowered fifth degree in minor mode; quasi-dominant or plagal effect

Berlioz: *Symphonie Fantastique,* fourth movement

c. Third-related minor triads alternating in symmetrical motive construction

Wagner: *Das Rheingold*

d. Minor triad on leading tone in minor mode replacing subdominant, or dominant in symmetrical motive layout

Debussy: Quartet in G minor, fourth movement

Permission for reprint granted by Durand et Cie, Paris, France, copyright owners; Elkan-Vogel Co., Inc., Philadelphia, Pa., agents.

e. Major triad on lowered fifth degree in major mode acting as replacement for subdominant in plagal cadence

Liszt: Sonata in B minor, final cadence

f. Shift from minor to major triad half step below with a pedal tone common to both chords

Brahms: *Tragic* Overture

Allegro non troppo

g. Juxtaposed triads used in succession

Dvorak: Symphony No. 5, fourth movement

Allegro con fuoco

Debussy: Quartet in G minor, Op. 10, fourth movement

Trés animé

Permission for reprint granted by Durand et Cie, Paris, France, copyright owners; Elkan-Vogel Co., Inc., Philadelphia, Pa., agents.

COLORISTIC CHORD ALTERATIONS

Among our previous encounters with color values in harmony we can refer to interchange of mode and to chromatically altered tones of melodic ornamentation. Many single instances of interchange of mode involved a moment of intensified harmonic color between two points of harmonic stability; the same may be said of altered neighbor tones, appoggiaturas, changing tones, passing tones, etc.

This process of inflection within the movement phase of a movement-arrival formula tended to become more elaborate and more frequently used in nineteenth-century music. Inflections were used in pairs, and entire chords were employed to create the coloristic nuance. Typically, such chords were seventh chords of one type or another, and in the majority of cases they incorporated at least one tritone, combining a harmonic drive along with the color content. The diminished seventh chords in measures 3, 4, 13, and 14 of Ex. 1*a* and the suspended dominant seventh chord with the raised fifth in measure 19 of the same example illustrate coloristic chord alterations involving seventh chords with tritone action. In the first two cases, the altered chord is part of the motive structure of the theme; in the second case, the alteration intensifies the cadential effect by making D♯ act in the manner of a leading tone.

One striking aspect of this process of altering chords of the seventh was that the alteration did not generally appear as a non-chord tone; it did not modify the chord so drastically that it no longer sounded like a typical seventh chord of the tonal harmonic vocabulary. Thus dominant and diminished seventh types, the augmented $\frac{6}{3}$, $\frac{6}{4}$ and $\frac{6}{5}$, the VII⁷ of the major mode, the augmented triad, the seventh with augmented fifth— these are the constructions arrived at by alteration, but they are *not* diatonic in the key in which they are used, and they are not employed strictly for cadential purposes, although they may function very well to achieve a cadential effect.

In the example below we give a number of progressions in which the middle chord is an altered construction of the type described above. The first and last chord represent the tonic of a key. In the parentheses the *type* of chord is indicated.

EX. 5.   Altered seventh chords

In Ex. 6, passages from music literature employing such chords within a diatonic framework are quoted:

EX. 6.   Altered seventh chords in music literature

a. V$\frac{4}{3}$, V$\frac{4}{2}$

Sibelius: Symphony No. 1 in D, second movement

Reprinted by permission of Breitkopf & Haertel, Leipzig, and Associated Music Publishers, Inc., New York, their United States representative.

b. VII^{7}b

Brahms: Symphony No. 3, first movement

c. II^7

Strauss: *Blinden Klage*

Copyright, 1906, Ed Bote & G. Bock, Berlin.

d. VII^7

Strauss: *Till Eulenspiegel*

e. VII^7

Bizet: *L'Arlésienne,* Suite 2

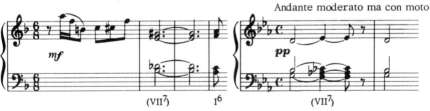

Much of the effect of the chromatic inflections we have discussed will depend on the general context of the piece itself. It is inconsistent to introduce one "purple" touch into a piece that is otherwise purely diatonic. We should build a "form" with these chromatic inflections in so far as using one requires matching it with others, as in Ex. 1 of this chapter. Practically speaking, chromatic inflections will be likely to appear to good advantage within a diatonic context at the following points:

1. With the first phase of harmonic movement. Heard within the first three or four chords, the inflection establishes the coloristic element for the piece. It can become a motive in its own right, inviting repetition, variation, or similar uses.

2. Within cadential areas, as an approach to, or part of, the half cadence or authentic cadence. Such treatment will presume some previous chromatic inflections.

In order to gain the full flavor of the chromatic inflection we should be particularly careful not to change harmony too quickly. In this style of music, therefore, we may expect a rather slow rate of chord change. We need at least four voices singing preferably in the more resonant registers, i.e., middle and low, in order to bring out the full coloristic effect of the harmony. Intense motivic play, give-and-take texture will reduce the purely coloristic value of a progression of this type. Therefore, a full chordal texture or a melody with an ornamental figured accompaniment will best project the coloristic chromaticism.

COLORISTIC KEY CHANGES

When we were studying interchange of mode, we had occasion to extend a period by means of a digression to a key related to the major tonic through its parallel minor. Thus, in C major, we may have visited Ab major, Eb major, or Db major in order to expand the tonic-minor or subdominant-minor areas. Although the main purpose of such digressions was structural expansion by means of a wider functional scope, still the immediate impact was that of a striking shift of harmonic color. These two aspects, *cadence* and *color,* can be manipulated so that their relative emphases vary greatly, much as we have observed in the treatment of single chromatic nuances. As we might expect, the tendency in the nineteenth century was strongly in the direction of highlighting the color value, while cadence action was often relegated to the role of accommodating interesting shifts of key. In Ex. 2*b* of this chapter there are striking shifts between G (as V of C) and Eb at measures 81 and 88, and Eb and C (as IV of G) at measure 92. The cadential aspects of these shifts are minimal (we have only the *gesture* of a cadence in the phrase structure and quasi-leading-tone action in several voices); the shift of color value is maximal and certainly makes the sense of the passage for the listener.

In the following set of examples striking shifts of tonal center highlight each passage. In Ex. 7*a,* a cadential drive sets in immediately following the shift and comprises the principal meaning of the remainder of the long period. In Ex. 7*b,* the color of two third-related triads is emphasized. Only at the very last moment do we realize that the second triad is a *dominant,* not a *tonic,* and that the progression has retained a vestige of the logic of the cadential formula. In keeping with these two contrasted treatments of harmonic chiaroscuro, Beethoven has saturated the first progression with expanded dominant action involving quick shifts of chord, while in the second progression he has allowed the sounds of single major triads to remain for twelve and twenty-eight measures, respectively, so that the harmonic color will permeate thoroughly.

EX. 7.   Cadential and coloristic shifts to distant tonal centers

a. To VI♭

Beethoven: Violin Concerto, Op. 61, first movement

b. To III$_{♯3}$

Beethoven: Symphony No. 6 in F major, first movement

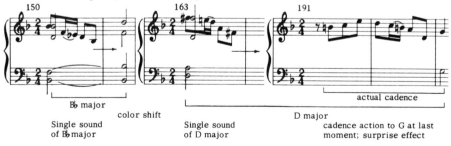

In a song or short instrumental piece the entire form can be outlined by coloristic key shifts. For optimum effect the melodic material should be lyric in quality with a frankly singing melodic line; texturally, a sonorous projection of the central harmonies of the key generally with a full setting gives body to the harmonies. Then, transposition of the harmonic continuity to a series of remote keys throws the melodic material into successively new lights, and permits the listener to enjoy rehearing of the original material without incurring the danger of redundancy or lack of harmonic interest. The return to the home key, often accomplished by the same tangential action as that used in the digressions, neatly rounds off the form. Chopin's Prelude in E major illustrates this harmonic type, and we quote it below in its entirety.

EX. 8.   Chopin: Preludes, Op. 28, No. 9 in E major

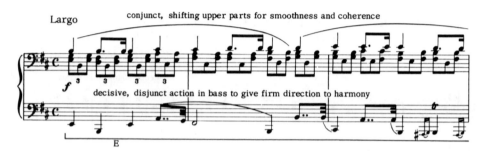

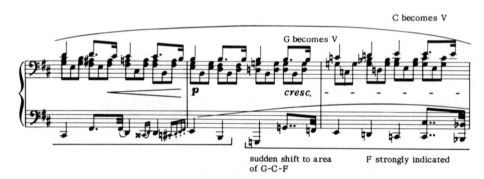

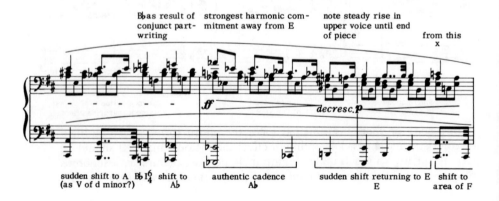

point choice of chord is influenced by rise in uppermost voice　　　cadential action

In Ex. 8 the very smooth stepwise shifts in the right hand enable the music to slide momentarily into chords from remote tonal areas. It is the remarkable firmness of the bass which moves by cadential leaps that causes the harmony to appear to make abrupt changes of tonal center.

Sections of larger compositions may contain effective coloristic key shifts. In the finale of his Concerto for Piano in E♭ major, Beethoven presents the principal theme of the movement successively in C major, A♭ major, and E major. This tour of third-related keys represents the principal digression section of the movement, corresponding to the development in a sonata-rondo form. Smetana prepares the final cadential section of his Overture to *The Bartered Bride* by making a huge digression away from the home key, F major, in the following manner:

Key	F	D♭	D	E♭	E	C as V of F	F
Measures	362–367	368–379	380–382	383–385	386–393	394–421	421 *et seq.*

A tremendous expansion of C minor as preparation for C major takes place in Schubert's Overture to *Rosamunde*. We quote the passage to the point of arrival at the dominant in order to show what dimensions the circle of keys has achieved in this piece.

EX. 9.　Schubert: Overture to *Rosamunde*

(*continued*)

296

sudden shift to E♭ major

E♭ major

interchange of mode; bass slips
down to I$^6_4$ of G♭ major

G♭ major

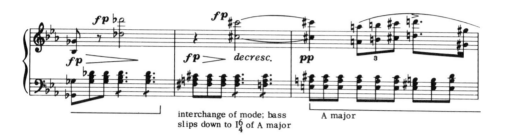

interchange of mode; bass
slips down to I$^6_4$ of A major   A major

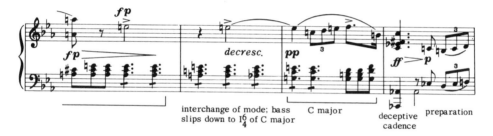

interchange of mode; bass   C major   deceptive   preparation
slips down to I$^6_4$ of C major   cadence

for V of C {minor / major}   V   harmony has come full circle
                                C

12 measures on V

Coloristic contrasts can also be used to create a three-part harmonic structure for a small composition; romantic composers have often used movement to a third-related key as a substitute for the dominant or relative minor. The Prelude in B♭ major of Chopin moves to G♭ major for the middle section; Brahms's *Romanze,* Op. 118, no. 5, moves through F major to D major to F major with some harmonic preparation for each section.

Approach to the new tonal center or degree may be made in several ways:

1. By moving directly to the new chord, as in Ex. 7*b*
2. By slipping the bass upward or downward, as in Ex. 8, measure 5
3. By preparing a cadence in the new key, as in Ex. 9, leading to measure 19
4. By a deceptive cadence in the home key, as in Ex. 7*a,* measure 28

SUMMARY

1. Chromatic digressions in diatonic harmony are principally used for coloristic purposes.
2. They include:
a. Juxtaposed triads belonging to different keys.
b. Altered seventh chords, often supplanting usual dominant harmony.
c. Coloristic key changes, which can provide a structural plan for a short composition or a section of a large work.
3. Smooth, conjunct part writing and full, compact texture are essentials for the effectiveness of chromatic digressions in diatonic harmony.

EXERCISES

1. Using the following basses for the opening motives, construct phrases which make use of chromatic digressions in diatonic harmony:

2. Write a short piece of sixteen or more measures in which the key scheme is as follows:

E♭ major, C♭ major, A♭ minor, A major, E major, E♭ major (or)
G major, B major, E♭ major, E major, C major, C minor, G major

Chapter Twenty-five

Coloristic Piano Texture

Exploration of sonority values went hand in hand with exploration of harmonic color in nineteenth-century music. The principal instrumental media for projecting sonority values, the piano and the orchestra, assumed their definitive structure in the nineteenth century. Greater range, color, and fullness of sound were available at this time than in the preceding century.

Certainly one of the most remarkable expansions in sonority values occurred in piano music. The modern sustaining-pedal action was perfected, enabling the piano to hold a tone effectively for a moment after the tone had been struck. Thus, the piano was able to perform "sostenuto" music in a style similar to that of wind and string instruments. Moreover, as the struck string vibrated, its vibrations set into motion all strings above it in pitch which corresponded to the partials of the struck tone's harmonic series. Thus, if middle C were struck, all Cs above it would sound faintly, Gs from an octave and a fifth above, Es from two octaves and a third, etc. The original sound would have, by virtue of the sustaining pedal, a subtle, pervasive aura of sound accompanying it. Properly projected, these sonority properties of the piano can be arresting, even hypnotic in effect.

While every nineteenth-century composer from Weber to Strauss explored color values in texture and evolved his own particular palette, it was Frédéric Chopin who was probably most committed to the values of color in his own medium, the piano, and who established the most definitive procedures for coloristic exploitation of that instrument. For our purposes, Chopin's music provides ideal models. Much of it consists of small pieces, built up quite symmetrically in so far as phrase and period structure are concerned. As a rule, one quality of sound is explored within a piece or within a principal section of a piece. Often there is a smoothly flowing, lyric melody that floats above the elaborate figuration in these pieces which project familiar song and dance values, such as the waltz, mazurka, nocturne, polonaise, etc. Chopin's Preludes, Op. 28, illustrate a great variety of pianistic textures. Some of these are analyzed below.

EX. 1.   Chopin: Preludes, Op. 28, No. 1 in C major

Each two-note melodic motive contains one non-chord tone. These prominent tones of figuration, systematically used, give a characteristic nuance
to the entire piece. At no time in Ex. 1 are more than two notes struck
together. The two uppermost voices and the bass comprise the essential
framework of the harmony, corresponding to the two elements of texture,
bass and treble, described earlier in this text.

EX. 2.   Chopin: Preludes, Op. 28, No. 2 in A minor

Three-note chords in accompaniment, distributed in alternating low and high intervals. Middle voice binds texture by becoming in turn the upper and lower tones of the alternating intervals.

EX. 3.   Chopin: Preludes, Op. 28, No. 5 in D major

Each level of the texture has a distinctive ⅜ figure of individual design, beginning at different points in the ⅜ measure. The three lowermost voices comprise the essential framework of the harmony.

EX. 4.   Chopin: Preludes, Op. 28, No. 8 in F♯ minor

Only two voices struck together at any time.

304

EX. 5.   Chopin: Preludes, Op. 28, No. 15 in D♮ major

Maximum of 3 voices {struck} together

EX. 6.   Chopin: Preludes, Op. 28, No. 20 in C minor

Texture exploits full harmony, 5–7 voices sounding simultaneously, low register of piano. Basic framework lies in bass and upper three voices, as a rule.

EX. 7.   Chopin: Preludes, Op. 28, No. 11 in B major

The separation of the levels of the texture suggests a chamber-music scoring. Actual sound comprises but two voices sounding together except at the beginning of each measure and all of measure 6.

In the examples we have used for illustration the principal features of nineteenth-century piano figuration are embodied. These include the following:

1. There is a basic three- or four-part chordal framework that carries out traditionally proper lines of voice leading. This framework consists, further, of two elements, a *bass line* and the *composite movement of the upper voices.*

2. Voices are added to fill in all or most of the chord spaces in the middle and upper registers; a seven- or eight-tone sonority is thus created. These added tones are doublings of the basic voices. Spacing of these sonorities tends to be wide in the lower registers, close in the upper registers, corresponding roughly to the spacing of the harmonic series.

3. These multitone sonorities are then spread out into some well-defined linear pattern of figuration, in which the tones succeed each other in a clearly marked *serial* order. Since we are dealing with sonority and not with independent part leading, it is possible to increase or decrease the number of tones in the complex and to change the figuration somewhat if chord make-up, voice leading, or texture requires modifications for good musical effect. The general sonority value and figuration pattern, at any rate, should not be changed in style.

4. In addition to its distinctive shape, the figuration generally contains some single element which provides a special color value. This may be systematic use of a salient non-chord element, such as a suspension, neighbor tone, changing tone, appoggiatura, or this element of color may consist of emphasis on a single chord tone by repetition or scoring; such a tone may be the fifth of the chord, which can highlight certain resonance values in the harmonic series of the chord.

5. Structurally, music which employs such figuration is not strongly concerned with development and expansion of period structure but rather is concerned with filling a period of musical time by means of a single value of color. Therefore, the quality of movement tends to be even and regular, with relatively little interruption of the basic flow. Then, in order to express itself, the figuration must be repeated relatively unchanged in different harmonies. This calls for motives of equal length, leading to a rather consistent regularity of two- and four-bar phrase structure. Very seldom do we discover disruptions of this regularity in order to make room for a broad cadence. Often, the cadence is incorporated into the regular phrase structure, and we may hear a *feminine* ending, in which the tonic chord appears at the last light part of a measure or measure group.

6. Above the texture, or embedded within it, a simple, appealing lyric melody proceeds. In the case of Chopin's work, the melodies have affinities with the melodic style of early nineteenth-century Italian opera, which, indeed, influenced Chopin strongly.

EXERCISES

1. Analyze texturally the compositions listed below, as follows:
   a. Reduction of first four to eight measures to basic chord progression
   b. Separation of texture into component levels

Chopin: Preludes in F♯ major, A♭ major, B♭ major, D minor
Brahms: Intermezzi, Op. 76, nos. 3, 4, 6
Beethoven: Sonata, Op. 31, no. 3, finale
Beethoven: Sonata, Op. 109, first movement
Schubert: *Moment Musicale,* Op. 94

2. Realize in four-part harmony the basses given below, and develop two or more textures for each in the following manner:

   a. Four-part harmony.

   b. Doubling to make seven or eight parts in middle and upper registers.

   c. Serialize the components of each chord, and retain the series for the entire progression; create a distinctive melodic shape for the series.

   d. Introduce a distinctive rhythm, modeled upon a dance type.

   e. Modify the figure to include a salient non-chord element.

   f. If feasible, underline one of the elements by doubling, pitch salience, or time values so as to create a definite melodic line.

Chapter Twenty-six

Concentrations
of Chromatic Harmony

Since the sixteenth century, music of all styles and forms has made use upon occasion of concentrations of chromatic harmony. The later Italian madrigalists, the keyboard-fantasy composers of the seventeenth and eighteenth centuries, and the composers who broadened the sonata form of the classical era—these are among the important musicians who dealt intensively at times with chromatic harmony. In some cases, the emphasis was placed upon coloristic effects; as a rule, the shift of harmonic focus was intended primarily to serve a structural purpose: to extend the key feeling and to act as a lever against the key. Drives within a key were enhanced by subsidiary-dominant action, often tightly packed, while movement outward through distant keys was powered by a series of cadential formulas.

In the following example, from the C-minor Fantasia of Mozart, K. 475, there are eight changes of harmonic direction or meaning in the nineteen measures quoted. The excerpt begins in C and returns, momentarily, to its dominant. Note that the elements which provide coherence within this shifting harmonic landscape are:

1. The conjunct bass line and the strong linear quality of the upper parts
2. The consistent texture
3. The regular repetition of motives

EX. 1.   Mozart: Fantasia in C minor, K. 475

Chord or progression: half cadence   IV$^6_{4\ 3}$ half cadence
Harmonic implications: C minor   Bb minor

(continued)

In this example virtually every chord participates in some kind of cadential formula or progression that resembles a cadential formula. Still, the change of harmonic meaning is so quick and tangential, the positions of the chords so light, and the rhetoric so continuous and nonperiodic that we lose much of the cadential sense and are carried along by the kaleidoscopic shifts of color and the linear movement. The cadential action is a disguised control, but the color value is the principal *appeal* of the passage.

We find this type of harmonic action in those parts of a large-scale classical movement which involve intense harmonic action and which can admit a certain degree of harmonic disorientation. These would be introductions, movements from one important key to another, and developments. This harmonic procedure is to be discovered only occasionally, and its large-scale structural purpose is to set off and emphasize important areas of harmonic stability.

In the nineteenth century concern with chromatic harmony came to dominate harmonic thinking; it appears quite clear that in the music of composers such as Liszt, Franck, and Wagner, ways and means of weakening and destroying the diatonic feeling were being sought. Harmony as a factor of structural orientation was becoming less and less clear. This saturation of chromaticism evolved quite logically from classical harmony, retaining many procedures and recognizing key relationships. It was simply the case of unstable elements gradually crowding out stable elements.

In order to obtain a clear view of the ways in which such concentrations of chromaticism were handled, we shall examine various aspects of the techniques involved. Much of the material has been covered in part during earlier chapters; the procedures are modified, and their importance changes in intensely chromatic action. It will give us a clear perspective of harmonic evolution in the nineteenth century to compare the respective roles of these procedures in key-centered versus key-obscured harmony. The procedures we shall cover are:

1. Chord vocabulary
2. The harmonic guideline
3. Progression of tonal centers
4. Structure, including rhythmic and melodic aspects

CHORD VOCABULARY

One of the most important controls in nineteenth-century chromaticism is the very sound of the harmony itself. Each chord, each sound is drawn from the common vocabulary of triads, sevenths, and ninths, diatonic or altered. Arbitrary combinations occur very rarely and in such cases can be rationalized as suspensions, appoggiaturas, etc. As we work in a chromatically saturated idiom we can help ourselves retain a harmonic focus by thinking of every combination as a *type*, such as major triad, minor triad, diminished or augmented triad, dominant seventh, diminished seventh, VII⁷, dominant seventh with raised or lowered fifth, major or minor dominant ninth, and the secondary seventh types. (See Chap. 24, page 290 *et seq.*)

Not only do these types provide related sonority and color resources from a large *family* of tone combinations, but also they enable us to establish key implications in order to build up the harmonic structure of a passage. The chromatic harmony of the nineteenth century is selected carefully, and its key schemes reveal a rational plan.

The Prelude in E minor by Chopin illustrates many characteristic aspects of nineteenth-century harmonic instability and chromaticism. We shall use it here as a model for the demonstration of the procedures to be described. First, we catalogue the chord types:

EX. 2.   Chopin: Preludes, Op. 28. No. 4, in E minor

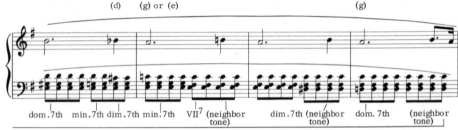

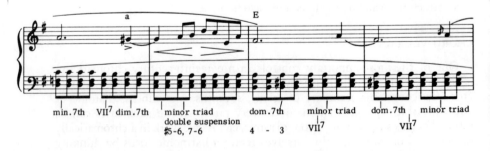

A bit of calculation will show that about three-quarters of the musical time in this piece is occupied with unstable or dissonant sound. Aside from several suspensions and one or two minor sevenths this instability is embodied in chord types which contain the sound of the tritone. Of these there are about a dozen of the type described here as the VII⁷, the minor seventh with the diminished triad from the lowermost note. It is the sound of this chord in many different contexts that gives a peculiarly unsettled and searching quality to nineteenth-century chromaticism. It crops up again and again in the music of Schumann, Liszt, Brahms, Wagner, Richard Strauss, and their contemporaries. Sometimes it acts as a dominant; sometimes as a subdominant; sometimes as a combination of altered tones whose identity as a chord and whose allegiance to a key are highly equivocal. In one of its disguises it is the famous *Tristan* chord, celebrated as representing the crisis, the saturation point of nineteenth-century chromatic harmony. The passage is given below:

EX. 3. Wagner: *Tristan und Isolde,* Prelude

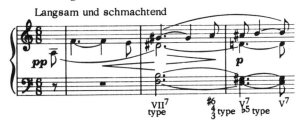

See also measures 6, 10, 12, 19, 25 for prominent use of VII⁷ type.

This passage also demonstrates nineteenth-century tendencies with respect to the kinds of unstable harmony used. VII⁷ types, dominant sevenths with raised or lowered fifths, dominant ninths—these are found in great abundance, particularly in Wagner's music, imparting striking colors and ambiguous tonal direction to the harmony. Compared to eighteenth-century harmonic exploration, which is cadential in manner and points clearly to whatever key is in question, nineteenth-century unstable harmony manipulates mutated dominants which neither yield up the key nor grasp it firmly.

THE HARMONIC GUIDELINE

From the beginning of our work we have relied on conjunct voice leading to provide a mechanical coherence to a harmonic progression; smooth connection of chords will confirm the sense of unity and balance that is inherent in cadential formulas.

When the key feeling is systematically undermined by chords that follow each other at tangents, tonally speaking, the responsibility of the part writing, the rhythmic action, and the general rhetorical effect to provide musical coherence become even greater. As the harmony becomes more centrifugal, some elements in the texture become more centripetal. In the majority of cases, the principal responsibility for holding the progression in line is assigned to the bass. Because of its weight of sonority and its prominence as the lower limit of the sound mass, the bass is best able to control the stability and direction of chord progressions. Any voice, bass or otherwise, which provides the linear factor of coherence acts as *a harmonic guideline*.

In Ex. 1 of this chapter the bass moves steadily by half steps for eighteen measures. At the nineteenth measure, when the harmony for a moment is stabilized on G major, the bass accomplishes this effect by the cadential leap of the perfect fourth. In Ex. 2, *all four* voices are involved in guideline action (and in Ex. 1 as well). In measures 12 and 13, 16, and 24 and 25 we have stronger cadential focus; the bass then moves by leap. We might formulate the relationship thus:

Harmonic movement—conjunct bass
Harmonic arrival—disjunct bass

Since so much nineteenth-century music circumvents harmonic arrival in order to avoid too emphatic a projection of key, it follows that conjunct bass movement will be an indispensable factor in this process.

PROGRESSION OF TONAL CENTERS

In organizing a progression of shifting chromatic harmonies the composer can retain his bearings by establishing a pattern of tonal centers. The *manner* in which these tonal centers are indicated is characteristic of the *chromatic* harmonic idiom, but very often the *plan* of degrees or keys carries out the logical progressions of *diatonic* tonal harmony.

In tonal harmony the sense of key is projected on the following levels of emphasis and clarity:

1. *Implied* or indicated by a *single chord,* tonic or dominant
2. *Indicated* or *established* by a *cadential formula*
3. *Confirmed structurally* in a *phrase* or *period*

Diatonic tonality employs all three levels to make the feeling of the key clear to the listener. Expanded cadential action or modulation operates to modify or intensify the sense of key. Chromatic harmony, assigning greater autonomy to levels 1 and 2, tends to obscure the clarity of key sense, to the point that a single chord of dominant function might be the only indication of a given tonal center in a phrase.

While the relative importance and functions of the various levels of key definition change in chromatic harmony, still the basic hierarchy of levels operates; moreover, the pattern of degree and tonal-center progression, when charted, often has cadential or sequential structure. For purposes of comparison, we give the following examples, which illustrate the methods by which the sense of A major can be projected on the several levels.

EX. 4.   Four projections of the sense of A major

a. A implied by tonic or dominant

b. A indicated, established by cadential formula

c. Confirmed structurally by cadential formulas, expanded cadential action, authentic cadence in a phrase

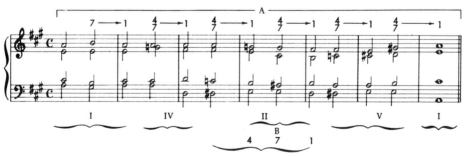

d. Circumscribed, alluded to, not strongly confirmed

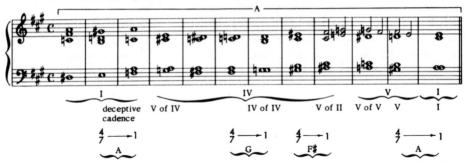

Lower brackets indicate complete cadential formulas; other combinations are not fully resolved.

In Exs. 4*a* and 4*b* there is no question of the sense of A major. In 4*c* there may be some concern between measures 3 and 5, but the structural level is confirmed at both the beginning and the end. In 4*d* we do not hear A until the every end, and at that point there is some doubt as to whether A is the tonic of its own key or the dominant of D; this is especially critical because of the strong commitment to G at measure 7, which causes A to be taken possibly as the V of D. Individual chords in this progression, forming a series of overlapping dominants, give us no clear clue as to the home key. The harmonic focus is blurred or, at least, so decentralized that it appears to point in two directions. Still, in the building of this progression we can see that A was the principal point of reference. The deceptive cadence to F major implies A, while the final cadence again indicates A. Then, if we take A as the reference, the large-scale cadential formula structure falls into place; the movement through the IV and V areas to I provides a logical, cadentially directed framework of degrees or implied tonal centers, as follows:

E A D G   F♯ B E A (D?)

Two circles of fifths, with each degree represented by either a dominant chord or a dominant-to-tonic progression, comprise the first level, i.e., the *implication* of key, in Ex. 4*d*.

In the Chopin Prelude in E minor the sense of E minor is clear at the beginning and at the half cadence and is confirmed finally at the end with broad rhetorical emphasis. In between there is much shifting and instability. Before the half cadence, A minor as IV of E becomes the target of a broad cadential formula. Other tonal centers are implied briefly. In the example (Ex. 2) the capital letter represents the home key, lower-case letters represent clearly projected tonal centers, and lower-case letters in parentheses represent tonal centers implied by each passing chord. You will observe that most of these shadowy degrees are closely related to E minor in the dominant, subdominant, or relative-major areas. Only the one chord implying G♭ is truly remote in feeling. (The notes of this chord are identical with those of the *Tristan* chord.)

The famous Prelude to *Tristan und Isolde* moves through three different degree or tonal-center patterns in its first two periods, comprising measures 1–24. We have:

Rising sequence in thirds with broad half cadences

A, measures 1–4.
C, measures 1–8.
E, measures 9–16; E becomes the V of A.

Closely spaced circle of fifths

First there is a deceptive resolution of the V of A to F major, which becomes in turn the IV of C leading to

G, measures 18 and 19 (as V of C).
C, measures 19 and 20.
F, measure 20 (implied through B♭), which immediately becomes

Cadential formula in A

D minor, measures 20–22.
E, measures 22 and 23 as V of A.
A, measure 24, *authentic cadence.*

Each of the degrees listed here is represented always by its dominant, less by tonic harmony. Again we see in this passage a rather closely related constellation of degrees, systematically ordered in several series.

The examples that follow illustrate concentration of chromatic harmony based upon patterns of tonal center involving the following relationships:

1. Circle of fifths downward
2. Circle of fifths upward
3. Circle of thirds upward
4. Circle of thirds downward
5. Diatonic stepwise movement upward
6. Diatonic stepwise movement downward
7. Chromatic stepwise movement upward
8. Chromatic stepwise movement downward
9. I–VI–II–IV–V–I cadential formula

Each of these patterns is worked out in two versions with four or five degrees, using in one version cadential formulas and in the other version overlapping dominants. Keys and symbols indicated in parentheses and brackets refer to implied keys and subsidiary cadential formulas.

EX. 5.   Nine patterns of tonal center

a. Circle of fifths downward

b. Circle of fifths upward

c. Circle of thirds upward

d. Circle of thirds downward

e. Diatonic stepwise movement upward

f. Diatonic stepwise movement downward

g. Chromatic stepwise movement upward

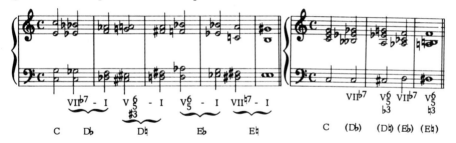

h. Chromatic stepwise movement downward

i. I–VI–IV–II–V–I cadential formula

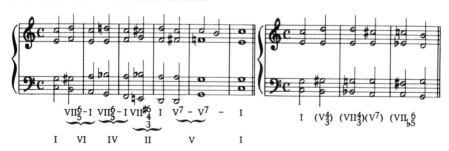

STRUCTURAL ASPECTS OF CHROMATIC HARMONY

Throughout this text we have associated harmony with structure. Key is embodied in phrases and periods built up by cadential formulas and symmetrical rhythmic relationships; by this process we are provided with a sense of broad organic coherence and clear direction. This is probably the most important single value of diatonic functional harmony.

Chromaticism works against this sense of harmonic clarity in structure. Often this is only eventually to strengthen the key sense by "recoil" effects; at other times, the sense of key is drastically weakened without compensating cadential confirmation. We cannot explore here the vast implications for structure which chromaticism has, but we shall look at some of its structural aspects as they affect period formation.

EX. 6.   Schumann: *Nachtstücke*, Op. 23, no. 2

Markiert und lebhaft

Example 6 is a perfectly symmetrical period, four measures in length. It possesses the following characteristics of standard period structure:

1. Home key, which is F major
2. Half cadence answered by authentic cadence
3. Phrase I repeated as phrase II with cadential modification
4. Characteristic style (bourrée, in this case)

However, Schumann has crammed as much chromaticism as possible into this brief structure. The treatment of the key and the cadences shows to what extent the harmony has centrifugal tendencies. We can note these points:

1. Both cadences appear only at the last instant in each phrase: the amount of time and rhythmic emphasis given to the key-defining gestures is very small.

2. Of the sixteen beats in this period, nine·are concerned with cadential formulas circling around III, VI, and II, degrees which are relatively farther from the tonic than IV or V. The "sound" of the period does not embody F major clearly.

3. Degree movement is downward by thirds in the unstable phases.

The regular period structure is part of this tug of war between chromaticism and the home key. The automatic points of arrival at the end of each phrase, weak as they may be, provide targets for the harmony to settle on the dominant and tonic. Chromaticism has pushed the tonic away from the position of control, with respect to both sound and time, but the tonic takes advantage of the absolute regularity to assert itself at the last moment.

Characteristically, Schumann builds periods with emphasis upon unstable, centrifugal, rhythmically light values. Often, the motives with which he builds up his phrases and periods have a feminine rhythmic pattern; in spite of the shifting chromaticism, the motives are generally repeated verbatim, supporting the sense of mechanical metric regularity. The following period moves from Bb major to F major; only at the last quarter note is the root of the F-major triad given to the bass. This constitutes a minimum of key emphasis.

EX. 7.   Schumann: *Novelettes,* Op. 21

Munter

In the Chopin Prelude in E minor, the period structure contains twenty-five measures instead of the normal eight or sixteen. Of these twenty-five, four additional measures are contained in an internal expansion of the first phrase, one additional measure is incorporated in the second phrase, and four measures make an extension of the cadence of the period. The part writing is so smooth and the action so continuous that it would be difficult to determine at just what point expansion takes place. Chromaticism makes the movement flow onward, to such points where the structure is clarified by cadential action. The bass here is a guide, moving from G down to B.

It would be possible to cite hundreds of examples in eighteenth- and nineteenth-century music in which harmonic digressions and explorations act to expand periods far beyond their normal length. One such period is that which opens the Quintet in C major, K. 515, of Mozart; it comprises sixty measures of which the first twenty represent the first phrase group that ends with the half cadence, while the next forty measures encompass the digressions and cadential reestablishment of the home key. The diagram below illustrates the harmonic continuity of this period:

EX. 8.   Period expanded by harmonic digression

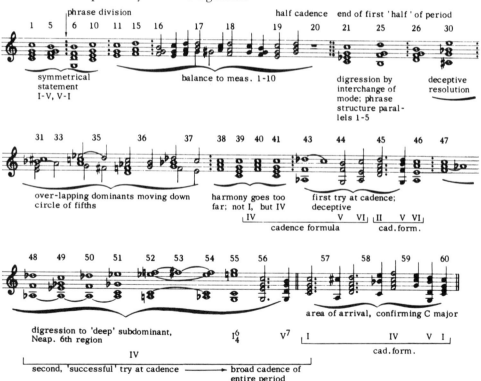

Chromaticism is used at times in the ostinato bass patterns of baroque and classical music. A familiar type is the descending conjunct bass line, moving between 8 and 5 of the scale and touching upon all intervening tones. This is a version of the *chaconne bass*. The bass repeats the short figure (four to eight measures in length) constantly while the upper voices vary the texture, melody, harmony, rhythm, and style. The last and first measures of the figure make an authentic cadence, while the middle measures move into a short-range harmonic digression. The *Crucifixus* from the B-minor Mass of Bach is a celebrated example of such an ostinato piece. As you examine the work, you will notice that at times Bach circumvented the authentic cadence indicated by the bass; chromaticism and instability, at these points, assume greater structural importance, holding the line of tension firm for two or three variations. Other examples of the chromatic chaconne bass are found in the Chaconne of the Solo Sonata for Violin of Bach in D minor, the Thirty-two Variations in C minor of Beethoven, and Dido's Lament from Purcell's *Dido and Aeneas*.

In the preceding examples the centrifugal movement of the chromatic harmony was held in line by cadential action which assumed control at various points in the periodic structure; also, a clear arrangement of statement and counterstatement between phrases (and motives) helped to organize the melodic material in a reasonable manner.

At times in eighteenth-century music and very often in the nineteenth century chromaticism took over control of the musical expression; consequently, structural premises were evolved that accommodated wandering harmony. These premises differed in many respects from the cadential, key-oriented symmetry of classical periodic structure. Yet, they possessed a logic which matched that of classical periodic structure, a logic which was applied, in the nineteenth century, with striking consistency by the composers who explored chromaticism deeply.

Since key definition, with its superstrong rhythmic accents at the authentic cadence, is necessarily eliminated in chromatic areas of action, other elements must move in to compensate for possible loss of coherence and unity. Chief among these is the treatment of *motivic material*.

In Exs. 1 and 2 of the present chapter a single motive is used repeatedly in a manner that would hardly be acceptable in straightforward, diatonic period structure. Indeed, in diatonic music we might well expect to find rather bold contrasts of motivic material within the first phrase. In the Mozart example, there are thirteen statements of the motive announced in the first measure; the Chopin contains nineteen statements of the opening motive. Both these motives are fashioned so that statement can be linked to following counterstatement in an unbroken chain. Each motive consists of a long tone preceded by an upbeat; a chain of iambic meters is the result, and there is no specific limit to the number of motives that may be thus linked. Structurally, then, the characteristic features of the melodic material in these examples are as follows:

1. The simple melodic figures give profile to the shifting harmonies.
2. The repetitions of melodic motives provide a tightening factor that secures the impression of unity.
3. The regular rhythmic patterns provide an even quality of movement and a proper spacing of the chord progression.

The structural chain thus fashioned is directed to specific melodic apices by upward or downward pitch movement; this movement is rarely straight but rather tends to describe an undulating pattern that modifies the overall rising or falling action. Thus, in the Mozart example, the overall descent is from C to F♯; there is an internal "wave" upward from A♭ to B after which the descent is directly to F♯. Each measure of the Chopin shows a small rise ornamenting the fall of the melody from B to F♯, in the first half. One further point about the Chopin: the left hand progression is based on a descending series of parallel sixth chords on G, F♯, F♮, E, D, C; this is an application of a *faux bourdon* technique. We can find many passages that exhibit the structural features described above in introductions to symphonies, exploratory sections in keyboard fantasias and preludes, development sections of sonata-form movements, and episodes in fugues and concerti grossi.

With this discussion of coloristic and chromatic harmony we have reached the end of our investigation of eighteenth- and nineteenth-century harmony. Beyond this point is the style of Richard Wagner; a study of his techniques would involve us in a new major area of musical composition. We should have to regard functional tonality and periodic structure in a much different perspective; we should have to acquire skill in a specialized manipulation of rhythmic and melodic motives; we should have to learn how to build the dynamic curve as a substitute for phrase and period structure. The chromaticism described in these latter chapters can be incorporated into the basic periodic-tonality framework. Within the limits set on one side by the simple 1–4–7–1 cadential formula to the period extended by means of chromatic explorations on the other side, we have been able to explore an interrelated group of topics; through these we acquired some skill in harmonic progression; we have also seen that structure and style are integral factors in harmonic action and color.

EXERCISES

1. Treat the given basses in the following manner:
    a. As they stand with diatonic cadential formulas.
    b. Introduce secondary dominants preceding degrees other than the tonic.
    c. Eliminate the chord of resolution for each of the secondary cadential formulas, or alter the chord of resolution so that it incorporates a tritone. Adjust the voice leading for maximum smoothness.
    d. Elaborate the texture in characteristic keyboard style, incorporating a repeated motive in the uppermost voice.

Chapter Twenty-seven

Summary

In this text we have tried to present a coherent and dynamic idea of harmony. We first established general points of reference, such as qualities of musical sound, qualities of musical movement and arrival. In the musical tradition of the past two centuries, these basic qualities have been embodied in the sense of key, the feeling for rhythmic statement and counterstatement, and the interaction of treble and bass elements in a texture.

For the sense of key, and indeed for virtually all the harmonic action described in this text, the 1–4–7–1 cadential formula was the central point of focus. Statement and counterstatement took the form of rhythmic and melodic motives gathered into phrases and periods. A skeletal texture of two parts was set up as the framework for part writing. Upon these first frames we began to elaborate. We filled out the texture and increased its inner activity; we augmented the chord vocabulary; we expanded the phrase and period structure; we introduced elements from other areas than the tonic and from the minor mode.

This process was a kind of troping, that is, elaborations and insertions upon an established model. Troping has taken place in Western music from the days of its origins to the present. Historically and esthetically, therefore, the approach carried out in this text can be justified. Eventually, we reached the level of rather elaborate two-part forms in our study of the growth of procedure and structure.

Throughout this text we have linked harmonic procedures to musical composition. This connection would be especially important for the music student whose principal interest is music theory or composition. Yet the approach can mean a great deal to the student who is mainly interested in musical performance. When he plays a sonata by Beethoven, an impromptu by Schubert, an étude by Chopin, or a concerto by Mozart, he will better appreciate the harmonic flow of the music by being sensitive to the various ways in which the 1–4–7–1 cycle of key definition is projected, how these relate to the structure of the work. He can thus better control his projection of harmonic action and arrival. In turn, this will inevitably reflect favorably upon the expressive qualities of his performance.

Our emphasis upon the creative and structural aspects has necessarily reduced the proportion of attention given to chord vocabulary. This would permit us to modify the chord vocabulary, perhaps to make drastic changes, without having to reshape the entire approach. The ideas of tonal center, structure, texture, melodic elaboration, and motive play which have been so integral a part of this approach can be of great value when work in modern harmony and composition is begun. The rhetoric of Stravinsky, Bartók, Hindemith, and indeed, Schönberg can become intelligible when seen as an evolution, a development from eighteenth- and nineteenth-century procedures. In the twentieth century, harmony makes decidedly less use of functional relationships, while melody loses much of its song and dance elegance; heightened rhythmic activity, sonority, and texture take on more responsibility in the musical process. An approach such as that presented in this book, which deals with general ideas of movement and arrival, statement and counterstatement, motive play, and the controlled opposition of soprano and bass, can provide a happy transition from preliminary studies in traditional styles to more advanced work with today's musical materials.

Index of Compositions Illustrated and Discussed

Subject Index